The seven sins
of
chocolate

The seven sins of chocolate

RECIPES BY LAURENT SCHOTT

PHOTOGRAPHS BY THOMAS DHELLEMMES
STYLING BY VÉRONIQUE VILLARET
EDITORIAL CONSULTANT PIERRE JASKARZEC

The seven

Sloth

• Tart à l'antillaise, 8 • Pear jam with chocolate, 10 •
• Warm chocolate cakes, 12 • Chocolate crêpes, 14 •
• Banana jam with chocolate, 16 • Floating islands, 18 •
• Bourdaloue tart, 20 •

Anger

• Fresh berry chocolate tart, 24 • Viennese chocolate cake, 26 •
• Crèmes brûlées flavored with Earl Grey tea, 28 •
• Black Forest gâteau, 30 • Spiced hot chocolate, 32 •
• Viennese chocolate sablés, 34 • Marble cake, 36 •

Lust

• Religieuses, 40 • Pears Belle-Hélène, 42 •
• Opera cakes, 44 • Raspberry chocolate tart, 46 •
• Chocolate savarins with vanilla cream, 48 •
• Chocolate mousse trilogy, 50 • Chocolate ice cream duo, 52 •

Pride

• Chocolate orange tuiles, 56 • Saint-Honoré, 58 •
• Profiteroles, 60 • Twelfth-Night cake, 62 •
• Chocolate macaroons, 64 • Kouglofs, 66 •
• Concorde, 68 • Mille-feuille, 70 •

sins of chocolate

Envy

Avarice

Gluttony

Secrets of the great chocolatiers

A glossary of terms can be found on page 63 of the booklet

Sloth

"Sloth is the beginning of vice."
—Dutch proverb

Tart à l'antillaise

This tart's tropical flavor provides the perfect end to an exotic meal.
Serve warm (by placing on a baking sheet in the oven for just 5 minutes), so that
the chocolate ganache is slightly runny, and add the finishing touch with a scoop
of rum-and-raisin ice cream and a glass of old dark rum.

Serves 6

SWEET PASTRY

3/4 cup all-purpose flour
2 tablespoons almond flour
2 tablespoons confectioners' sugar
Pinch of salt
6 tablespoons (3/4 stick) unsalted butter, chilled and sliced
1 large egg yolk beaten with 2 tablespoons ice water

Mix the flour, almond flour, confectioners' sugar, and salt in a medium bowl. Add the butter and rub between your fingertips until the mixture resembles coarse crumbs. Stirring with a large fork, add just enough of the yolk-water to evenly moisten the mixture—it should hold together when pressed between your finger and thumb. You may need a bit more water. Gather up the dough and press into a thick disk. Wrap in plastic wrap and refrigerate at least 2 and up to 12 hours.
Place the chilled dough on a lightly floured surface and rap all over with a rolling pin until malleable. Dust the top of the dough with flour and roll into a 1/8-inch thick round. Fit the dough into a 9-inch tart pan with a removable bottom, being sure it is snug at the corners. Roll the pin over the pan to cut off the excess dough. Prick the pastry all over with a fork. Refrigerate or freeze the dough-lined pan for 30 minutes.
Preheat the oven to 375°F. Place the tart pan on a baking sheet. Line the pan with a round of baking parchment. Fill the parchment with baking weights or dried beans. Place the pan on a baking sheet. Bake 10-12 minutes, until the dough is set. Lift off the paper with the weights and set aside. Continue baking until the crust is golden brown, about 10 minutes more. Remove from the oven and cool completely.

CHOCOLATE GANACHE

3 1/2 oz bittersweet chocolate, chopped
1/2 cup heavy cream
2 tablespoons unsalted butter, at room temperature

Place in a heatproof bowl. Bring the cream to a boil, pour onto the chocolate, and whisk until all the chocolate has melted. Add the butter, a piece at a time, mixing well until smooth.
Spread the ganache over the cooled tart base and chill in the refrigerator until set, about 30 minutes.

FLAMBÉED BANANAS

3 bananas
2 tablespoons unsalted butter
2 tablespoons soft brown sugar
2 tablespoons dark rum

Peel the bananas and cut into 1/4-inch thick rounds. Heat the butter in a large skillet until it turns a nut-brown color. Add the bananas and fry, turning them once, for 1–2 minutes, until the bananas are a light golden color. Add the sugar and rum, ignite, and set aside to cool. Arrange the bananas neatly on the chilled ganache base.

TO SERVE

Bittersweet chocolate shavings

Just before serving, remove the sides of the pan, and decorate the tart with a few shavings of chocolate.

Pear jam with chocolate

You'll need firm, juicy pears to make this jam. To test for setting, remove the pan from the heat and put a teaspoon of jam on a chilled saucer for a minute or two—a skin should form which wrinkles when pushed with the finger. If not, return the pan to a boil and test again at short intervals. For extra flavor and more visual impact, slip a piece of vanilla bean into each jar before covering. This jam is delicious with fresh crusty bread for breakfast or on plain rolls and cake for a snack. It will keep for up to a year if stored in a cool, dry place away from the light.

Makes approximately 8 x 8 oz jars

$2^3/_4$ lb ripe pears, peeled and cored ($2^1/_2$ lb after preparation)
$3^1/_2$ cups granulated sugar
juice of 1 lemon
7 oz bittersweet chocolate, chopped
2 vanilla beans, split open

Finely chop the pears. Place in a large wide saucepan with the sugar, lemon juice, and vanilla beans. Bring to a boil, stirring gently, then boil rapidly until the setting point is reached, as described above.
Add the chocolate, bring back to a boil, and remove the vanilla beans.
Pour into sterilized jars and cover with lids while still hot. Turn the jars upside down and cool.

Warm chocolate cakes

The best thing about these cakes is their soft, melting texture. Another benefit: they look complex, but are simple to prepare. You can even freeze the uncooked cakes if you want to—just allow a bit longer for baking. They are particularly delicious served with a swathe of berries and pistachio ice cream.

Serves 6

CHOCOLATE CAKES
3¹/₂ oz bittersweet chocolate, chopped
7 tablespoons (³/₄ stick + 1 tablespoon) unsalted butter, softened
2 large eggs, at room temperature
¹/₃ cup granulated sugar
¹/₂ cup all-purpose flour
1¹/₂ tablespoons unsweetened cocoa powder
¹/₂ teaspoon baking powder

Melt the chocolate in a microwave or in a heatproof bowl set over a pan of barely simmering water (the bowl must not touch the water). Remove from the heat and whisk in the butter until it has completely melted and the ingredients are well combined.
Whisk the eggs well with the sugar and add to the chocolate mixture. Sift in the flour, cocoa, and baking powder, and mix together using a wooden spoon.
Grease six 3¹/₄-inch ramekins and pour in the batter. Chill in the refrigerator for 1-4 hours.

PISTACHIO ICE CREAM
2 cups milk
³/₄ cup heavy cream
1 cup granulated sugar
7 large egg yolks
¹/₃ cup pistachio paste

Put the milk, cream and ¹/₂ cup sugar in a pan and bring to a boil. Beat the egg yolks in a bowl with the remaining ¹/₂ cup sugar and whisk in the hot milk and cream.
Return the mixture to the pan over low heat and cook, stirring constantly, until the custard thickens and coats the back of a wooden spoon. Strain through a wire strainer. Whisk in the pistachio paste. Cool in the refrigerator, stirring from time to time. Churn in an ice-cream maker. Store in the freezer.

RASPBERRY COULIS
1 cup raspberries, puréed and strained to remove the seeds
2 tablespoons granulated sugar
juice of 1 lemon

Mix all the ingredients together well and chill in the refrigerator.

TO BAKE AND ASSEMBLE THE CAKES
2 cups mixed berries, such as raspberries, blackberries, and blueberries
confectioners' sugar

Preheat the oven to 400°F.
Bake the cakes for 8-10 minutes. They should be just set on the outside, but soft and melting on the inside.
Decorate one side of each plate with a spoonful of raspberry coulis and add a swathe of berries. Turn out the cakes from the ramekins, dust with confectioners' sugar, and place next to the coulis. Add a scoop of pistachio ice cream to each plate and serve immediately.

Chocolate crêpes

These light, thin crêpes can be wrapped around a scoop of vanilla ice cream and flambéed with rum, filled with pistachio ice cream and crushed berries, or simply sprinkled with white sugar. Just make sure they're properly cooked, as their color can be deceptive. For added elegance, serve these pancakes filled and tied in bundles.

Makes about 16 crêpes

2 cups milk
3 oz bittersweet chocolate, chopped
1¹/₂ cups all-purpose flour
3 tablespoons Dutch-processed cocoa powder
3 large eggs, at room temperature
¹/₃ cup granulated sugar
pinch of salt
2 tablespoons unsalted butter
3 tablespoons dark rum

Warm the milk. Melt the chocolate in a microwave or in a heatproof bowl set over a pan of barely simmering water (the bowl must not touch the water). When the chocolate has melted, stir in half the milk.

Blend the rest of the milk along with the flour, cocoa, eggs, sugar, and salt in an electric blender. Melt the butter and add to the blender, along with the rum and melted chocolate mixture, and blend once more.

Chill the batter in the refrigerator for at least 3 hours. Heat a 7 to 8 inch nonstick skillet over medium heat until hot. Using about ¹/₄ cup of batter for each crêpe, pour the batter into the skillet and immediately tilt the skillet until the batter coats the bottom. Fill in any holes or gaps with drops of batter. Cook the crêpe until the edges are dried and the top looks set, about 1 minute. Lift up the edge with a heatproof spatula and turn the crêpe over. Cook until the crêpe is cooked through but pliable, about 30 seconds. Transfer to a plate. Continue with the remaining batter, separating the crêpes with pieces of waxed paper.

Banana jam with chocolate

This versatile jam is as at home on the breakfast table as it is served with chocolate macaroons and a cup of café au lait. It keeps perfectly well if stored in a cool, dry place away from the light. For a more intense taste, use really ripe bananas.

Makes approximately 8 x 8 oz jars

2¼ lb bananas
3½ cups granulated sugar
juice of 1 lemon
6 oz bittersweet chocolate, chopped

Peel the bananas and cut into rounds. Place in a large, wide saucepan with the sugar and lemon juice.
Bring to a boil, stirring gently, then boil rapidly until the setting point is reached. (To test for setting, remove the pan from the heat and put a teaspoon of jam on a chilled saucer for a minute or two—a skin should form which wrinkles when pushed with the finger. If not, return the pan to a boil and test again at short intervals.)
Add the chocolate to the pan and bring back to a boil.
Pour into jars and cover with lids while still hot.
Turn the jars upside down and leave to cool completely.

Floating islands

This recipe is a variation of a classic French dessert, *oeufs à la neige*, and is guaranteed to delight chocolate lovers and gourmets alike. The chocolate crème anglaise can be made with the milk used to poach the egg whites.

Serves 6

FLOATING ISLANDS
6 large egg whites, at room temperature
1/2 cup granulated sugar
2 1/2 cups milk

Whisk the egg whites until they form stiff peaks, gradually incorporating the sugar about halfway through the process.
Heat the milk in a wide saucepan until it simmers.
Use two spoons or an ice-cream scoop to add large scoops of egg white to the milk.
Poach for 3–4 minutes, turning half way through.
Remove the "islands" from the pan and let cool and drain on a clean kitchen towel. Do not discard the milk—it can be used to make the chocolate crème anglaise.

CHOCOLATE CRÈME ANGLAISE
5 oz bittersweet chocolate, chopped
2 1/2 cups milk
2/3 cup granulated sugar
2 vanilla beans, split open
6 large egg yolks

Place the chocolate in a heatproof bowl.
Put the milk, half the sugar, and the vanilla beans into a pan and bring to a boil.
Remove from the heat and let infuse for 15 minutes.
Whisk the egg yolks with the rest of the sugar in a bowl.
Bring the vanilla-flavored milk back to a boil, remove the vanilla beans and pour onto the egg mixture, whisking continuously.
Return the mixture to the pan and cook over low heat, stirring constantly, until the custard thickens and coats the back of a wooden spoon. Pour the hot custard through a wire strainer onto the chopped chocolate and whisk until the chocolate has melted.
Cool in the refrigerator.

TO ASSEMBLE THE DESSERT
Unsweetened cocoa powder
1 teaspoon chopped pistachio nuts

Pour the chocolate crème anglaise into individual dishes or glass bowls, and top each one with a floating island. Dust with cocoa powder and sprinkle with a few chopped pistachios.

Bourdaloue tart

The original Bourdaloue tart was invented in the early 20th century by a French pastry cook, whose shop was located on the Rue Bourdaloue, in Paris. Although you can make this version of the classic recipe using other fruit (apricots or bing cherries are good), it is best to use fresh pears. In season, they are even tastier when poached in vanilla syrup.

Serves 6

SWEET PASTRY
see page 8

Following the instructions on page 8, bake the pastry-lined tart pan for 10 minutes, just until the pastry is set. Remove the baking parchment and weights. Set the pastry base aside.

CHOCOLATE FRANGIPANE
6 tablespoons (^{3}/4 stick) unsalted butter, at room temperature
^{1}/2 cup almond flour
3 tablespoons granulated sugar
1 large egg yolk
1 tablespoon cornstarch
1 tablespoon dark rum
2 oz bittersweet chocolate, chopped

Beat the butter with an electric mixer on high speed until fluffy. Add the ground almonds, sugar, and beaten egg, and mix well. Then stir in the cornstarch and rum. Melt the chocolate in a microwave or in a heatproof bowl set over a pan of barely simmering water, add to the almond mixture, and mix well. Spread the frangipane over the base of the precooked pastry case.

TO BAKE AND ASSEMBLE THE TART
6 canned pear halves in syrup, drained well
toasted slivered almonds (optional)

Preheat the oven to 350°F.
Slice the pears about ^{1}/8-inch thick and arrange in concentric circles on the frangipane, pressing down lightly. Bake for 25–30 minutes. Cool in the tart pan for a few minutes, then remove and leave to cool completely on a wire rack. Remove the sides of the pan and serve.

Anger

"Anger, far sweeter than trickling
drops of honey, rises in the bosom
of a man like smoke."

—Homer

Fresh berry chocolate tart

Decadent in both appearance and flavor, the slightly sharp taste of the berries in this tart perfectly complements the bittersweet chocolate. For a more innovative version of this dessert, use hulled raspberries arranged on their tips, and add a drop of balsamic vinegar to each little "fruit cup" to intensify the flavor. Serve with a glass of port or strong, red wine.

Serves 6

SWEET PASTRY
see page 8

Following the instructions on page 8, bake the pastry-lined tart pan until the pastry is golden-brown, about 20 minutes. Cool completely.

CHOCOLATE GANACHE WITH RASPBERRIES
4 oz bittersweet chocolate, chopped
1/4 cup heavy cream
1/2 cup raspberries, rubbed through a fine-meshed wire sieve to remove the seeds
2 tablespoons unsalted butter, thinly sliced and chilled

Place the chocolate in a heatproof bowl.
Bring the cream and crushed raspberries to a boil in a small saucepan. Pour onto the chocolate. Whisk until the chocolate has melted, then add the butter, piece by piece, until the butter is melted.
Spread the ganache over the cooled pastry base and chill in the refrigerator for 30 minutes, just until beginning to set.

TO ASSEMBLE THE TART
10-12 strawberries
3 tablespoons red currant jelly
1 1/2 cups mixed berries, such as raspberries and blackberries, and stemmed red currants, if available
10 cherries, pitted
fresh mint leaves
chocolate shavings (optional)

Halve the strawberries and arrange on the tart, cut side up. Warm the jelly and brush over the strawberries. Fill the spaces with the other berries. Refrigerate until the filling sets, about 30 minutes more.
Top with cherries. Decorate with fresh mint leaves and chocolate shavings, if desired. Remove the sides of the pan and serve.

Viennese chocolate cake

This cake is one of the true glories of the Viennese pastry art. The original recipe for sachertorte (literally, "Sacher's cake") remains a closely guarded secret by the Hotel Sacher, but our recipe contains many of its delicious components, including a well-textured sponge and a shiny chocolate covering. Remember to remove it from the refrigerator 3 hours before serving as the combination of chocolate ganache and apricot jam is best appreciated at room temperature.

Serves 6

CAKE
1/3 cup + 1 tablespoon cake flour
3 tablespoons Dutch-processed cocoa powder
3 large eggs, separated, plus 1 large egg white, at room temperature
1/2 cup granulated sugar
3 tablespoons unsalted butter

Preheat the oven to 350°F. Grease and flour a 6-inch cake pan.
Sift the flour and cocoa into a bowl. Whisk the egg yolks with 1/3 cup of the sugar until they are light and frothy. Using an electric mixer, beat the egg whites until they form stiff peaks, adding the rest of the sugar half way through the process.
Melt the butter and cool slightly. Gently fold in a third of the egg whites to the beaten egg mixture with a rubber spatula. Then add the melted butter and the flour mixture. Finally, fold in the rest of the egg whites.
Pour the mixture into the pan and bake for about 30 minutes, until cake springs back when pressed. Remove from the pan and cool on a wire rack. When cool, slice the cake horizontally into 3 layers of equal thickness.

CHOCOLATE GANACHE
7 oz bittersweet chocolate, chopped
2/3 cup heavy cream
4 tablespoons (1/2 stick) unsalted butter, diced and softened

Melt the chocolate in a microwave or in a bowl set over a pan of barely simmering water (the bowl must not touch the water).

Bring the cream to a boil, and pour the cream onto the melted chocolate. Whisk until smooth, then add the butter, one piece at a time, whisking well until smooth. Refrigerate until the ganache is as thick as pudding.

TO ASSEMBLE THE CAKE
apricot jam, warmed

Spread each of the three cake layers with a thin layer of apricot jam. Spread a third of the chocolate ganache over the jam on each layer, up to the edges, but not over. Stack the layers into a single cake. Cut a strip of baking parchment to the depth of the cake by the circumference of the cake, plus an inch or two. Wrap the strip around the cake, fastening the overlap with a piece of tape to hold the layers firmly in place while chilling.
Chill in the refrigerator for at least 5 hours.

CHOCOLATE ICING
4 oz bittersweet chocolate, chopped
1/4 cup water
2 teaspoons glycerine
3/4 cup sifted confectioners' sugar, as needed

Melt the chocolate with the water, beat in the glycerine and sufficient sugar to achieve a coating consistency. Cool until pourable, but not too runny, or it will not adhere well to the sides of the cake.
Remove the paper strip. Place the cake on a wire rack set over a baking sheet. Smooth the icing over the top and sides of the cake with a metal spatula, and return to the refrigerator to set.

Crèmes brûlées flavored with Earl Grey tea

The citrus-flavored tea adds a sophisticated touch to classic crèmes brûlée. Serve as soon as the tops of the custards have caramelized, so that the cold cream highlights the warm, crunchy texture of the topping. If possible, caramelize using a kitchen blowtorch rather than under the broiler. Start to make the dessert the day before caramelizing so that the cream part sets well.

Serves 6

3/4 cup milk
3–4 Earl Grey tea bags
9 oz milk chocolate, chopped
6 large egg yolks
1 3/4 cups heavy cream
3 tablespoons turbinado crystallized (raw) sugar

Bring the milk to a boil, add the tea bags, remove from the heat, and set aside to infuse for 5 minutes. Remove the tea bags, pass through a wire strainer and bring back to a boil. Place the chocolate in a heatproof bowl. Pour onto the chopped chocolate and whisk briskly until the chocolate has melted.

Preheat the oven to 275°F. Beat the egg yolks and add to the chocolate-and-milk mixture, then add the cream. Divide the mixture between six 4-inch diameter custard cups or crème brûlée dishes. Place in a roasting pan filled with hot water to come halfway up the cups, and bake in the oven for 30–40 minutes or until the custards have set.Chill in the refrigerator overnight, or for at least 6 hours.
Sprinkle each custard with 1/2 tablespoon sugar, and caramelize with a blowtorch or under a very hot broiler. Serve immediately.

Black Forest gâteau

This Black Forest gâteau, inherited from the culinary tradition of Germany, doesn't give anything away—its impressive exterior conceals layers of incredibly light Genoise cake and frothy whipped cream flavored with kirsch. This is a truly splendid dinner party dessert or a delightful, afternoon indulgence with a cup of coffee.

Serves 6

CHOCOLATE GENOISE
3 large eggs
1/2 cup granulated sugar
3/4 cup cake flour
2 tablespoons Dutch-processed cocoa powder

Preheat the oven to 350°F. Butter and flour an 8 x 2 inch cake pan. Line the bottom of the pan with waxed or baking parchment.
Whisk the eggs and sugar together. Place the bowl over a pan of barely simmering water and continue to whisk with an electric mixer until the mixture is hot and frothy. (Do not allow the bowl to touch the water or the eggs may "scramble.") Remove the bowl from the pan and beat with the wire whisk attachment on high speed, until it is tripled in volume.
Sift the flour and cocoa into a bowl and carefully fold into the egg mixture with a rubber spatula.
Spread the batter into the pan and bake for about 30 minutes. To check that the cake is cooked, insert a wooden toothpick into the center—it should come out clean. Turn the cake out onto a wire rack, remove the waxed paper, turn right side up, and cool.

WHIPPED CREAM WITH KIRSCH
1 3/4 cups heavy cream
2 1/2 tablespoons granulated sugar
2 tablespoons kirsch

Beat the cream and sugar until the cream is somewhat stiff, the texture of a firm mousse. Add the kirsch and mix carefully. Chill in the refrigerator.

SYRUP
2/3 cup granulated sugar
1/3 cup water

Bring the sugar and water to a boil over high heat, stirring to dissolve the sugar. Cool the syrup to room temperature.

TO ASSEMBLE THE CAKE
4 tablespoons kirsch
1 (14-oz) can dark cherries in syrup
3 1/2 oz dark chocolate, in one piece
(you will not use it all)
Dutch-processed cocoa powder

Mix the syrup with the kirsch and drain the cherries. Slice the cake horizontally into 3 layers of equal thickness. Drizzle one of the layers with one-third of the kirsch-syrup, spread with a layer (1/2 inch) of whipped cream, and dot with half of the cherries (reserve the rest for decoration). Top with the second layer, drizzling with the remaining kirsch-syrup and spreading with whipped cream and then cherries. Top with the final layer and drizzle with the remaining syrup.
Completely cover the gateau with the rest of the whipped cream, smoothing the surface with a metal spatula. Cut shavings from the bar of chocolate with a sturdy vegetable peeler and use to decorate the cake, pressing lightly into the cream. Dust with cocoa powder and decorate with cherries. Chill in the refrigerator until ready to serve.

Spiced hot chocolate

With its smooth, creamy texture and delicate flavor, this twist on a cold-weather favorite is a pure, indulgent delight. For extra sweetness, top with a swirl of Chantilly cream on top and sprinkle with cocoa powder.

Serves 4

9 oz bittersweet chocolate, chopped
3½ cups milk
¾ cup heavy cream
2 cinnamon sticks
1 vanilla bean, split open
¼ cup packed light brown sugar

Place the chocolate in a heatproof bowl.
Put the milk, cream, cinnamon sticks, and vanilla bean in a pan and bring to a boil. Remove from the heat, set aside to infuse for 10 minutes, and then bring back to a boil. Remove the cinnamon sticks and vanilla bean. Pour the milk carefully onto the chocolate, whisking briskly. Stir in the brown sugar and serve piping hot.

Viennese chocolate sablés

These delicate cookies have a light, crumbly texture that makes them the perfect coffee time snack. Store in an airtight tin, in a cool dry place.

Makes 30–35 small cookies

12 tablespoons (1 1/2 sticks) unsalted butter, at room temperature
1 1/3 cups all-purpose flour
1/2 cup confectioners' sugar, plus extra for decoration
3 tablespoons Dutch-processed cocoa powder
1 egg white
pinch of salt

Preheat the oven to 375°F. Cover a baking sheet with baking parchment. Beat the butter, flour, confectioners' sugar, cocoa, egg white, and salt in a medium bowl with an electric mixer on medium speed until smooth. Using a pastry bag with a 1/2-inch wide fluted tip, pipe the mixture in 1-inch lengths (or larger zig zags) onto the baking sheet. Bake for about 12 minutes, until set. Cool on the sheet for a few minutes before transferring to a wire rack and dusting with confectioners' sugar. Cool completely.

Marble cake

This easy-to-make cake is ideal for brightening up a picnic basket. For added flavor, this recipe uses small pieces of candied orange, but you can replace the orange with other candied fruits or dried fruit soaked in rum. Just remember to take all the ingredients out of the refrigerator a few hours before making the cake—that way the batter will be perfectly smooth.

Serves 6–8

1/2 cup candied oranges or orange peel, diced
1/4 cup Grand Marnier
1 1/2 cups all-purpose flour
12 tablespoons (1 1/2 sticks) unsalted butter
3/4 cup granulated sugar
3 large eggs, at room temperature
1 teaspoon baking powder
3 tablespoons Dutch-processed cocoa powder

Preheat the oven to 350°F. Butter and flour a 6 cup fluted-tube pan.
Place the pieces of candied orange in a bowl and pour in 2 tablespoons of the Grand Marnier. Set aside to soak.

Mix the flour, butter, sugar, eggs, and baking powder in a heavy-duty electric mixer on medium speed until very smooth, about 3 minutes. Add the soaked oranges and mix for another 5 seconds. Divide the batter in half, add the cocoa to one half, and mix well.
Drop alternate, irregular portions of the two cake mixtures into the pan to create a marbled effect.
Bake for 45–50 minutes. Check that the cake is done by inserting a wooden toothpick into the center. When it comes out dry, remove the cake from the oven.
Turn out onto a wire rack, place a plate underneath the rack, and drizzle the cake with the remaining 2 tablespoons of Grand Marnier. Cool completely.

Lust

"I know of nothing that stimulates my stomach and excites my mind more voluptuously than the aromas of these delicious dishes as they caress the imagination and arouse feelings of desire."

—*La Nouvelle Justine ou les Malheurs de la Vertu*

Religieuses

Chocolate religieuses are the French pastry chef's anwer to the sin of indulgence.
Their name comes from the color of the frosting, which resembles a nun's habit.
To fully appreciate the smooth creaminess of the chocolate filling and
the lightly melting texture of the choux pastry, leave at room temperature for
a few minutes before serving.

Makes 6 religieuses

CHOUX PASTRY

1/2 cup water
1/2 cup milk
8 tablespoons (1 stick) unsalted butter,
cut into small pieces
1 teaspoon granulated sugar
1/4 teaspoon salt
1 cup all-purpose flour
4 large eggs

Bring the water, milk, butter, sugar, and salt to a boil in
a saucepan. Remove the pan from the heat and add all
of the flour. Beat with a wooden spoon over low heat
for about 1 minute until the dough forms a smooth,
thick paste. Transfer to a bowl and stir in the eggs one
at a time, making sure you stir each one in well before
adding the next.
Preheat the oven to 375°F. Cover baking sheet with
baking parchment. Using a pastry bag fitted with a
plain 1/2-inch tip, pipe 6 small balls (about the size of
a walnut) for the tops, and 6 large balls (about 2–2 1/2
inches in diameter) for the "bodies" of the religieuses.
Discard the remaining dough or pipe and bake more
balls to freeze for another use.
Bake for 25-30 minutes (the larger ones will take
longer), until they are golden brown and crisp. Cool
completely.

CHOCOLATE PASTRY CREAM

3 1/2 oz bittersweet chocolate, chopped
1 1/4 cups pastry cream (see recipe on page 5
of the booklet)
1/4 cup heavy cream

Stir the chocoate into the warm pastry cream. Let stand
until the chocolate melts. Add the heavy cream and
whisk until smooth.
Transfer the pastry cream to a pastry bag fitted with a
3/8-inch fluted tip. Pierce a small hole in the base of
each ball, and fill with the cream.

CHOCOLATE ICING

1 1/2 teaspoons powdered gelatin
2 tablespoons water
1 cup granulated sugar
3/4 cups Dutch-processed cocoa powder
3/4 cups heavy cream

Soak the gelatin leaves in cold water. Bring the sugar,
cocoa, cream, and remaining water to a boil in a
saucepan. Cook over low heat for 5 minutes, stirring
continuously, until slightly reduced. Remove from the
heat, add the softened gelatin, and stir well to dissolve
the gelatin. Cool until the icing is tepid.

TO ASSEMBLE THE RELIGIEUSES

1 cup chocolate icing (see recipe above)
silver drageés, for decoration

Warm the icing in a microwave (or a very low oven)
until tepid and liquid. Dip the top half of each choux
into the icing, turn the right way up and cool slightly.
Place the small choux ("heads") on the larger ones
("bodies") and top each with a drageé while the icing is
still soft.

Pears Belle-Hélène

Pears poached in syrup, vanilla ice cream, and hot chocolate sauce make this desert impossible to resist. To allow the flavors to develop fully, let the vanilla beans infuse overnight in the milk to be used for making the ice cream. If you prefer, you can make the dessert with chocolate ice cream instead of vanilla.

Serves 6

PEARS POACHED IN VANILLA SYRUP

6 firm, ripe Bosc pears
juice of 1 lemon
1 quart water
3/4 cup granulated sugar
1 vanilla bean, split open

Peel and halve the pears lengthwise, and remove the core. Dip quickly in the lemon juice to prevent them from discoloring.
Bring the water, sugar and vanilla bean to a boil in a saucepan.
Add the pears to the syrup and simmer gently over low heat for 15–20 minutes or until cooked through. Do not let them overcook—they should remain slightly firm when pierced with the tip of a small, sharp knife.
Cool in the syrup.

VANILLA ICE CREAM

2 cups milk
3/4 cup heavy cream
3/4 cup granulated sugar
2 vanilla beans, split open
7 large egg yolks

Bring the milk, cream, half the sugar, and the vanilla beans to a boil in a saucepan. Remove from the heat and set aside to infuse for 20 minutes.
Whisk the egg yolks with the remaining sugar until the mixture lightens in color. Remove the vanilla beans and slowly whisk the hot milk into the egg mixture.
Return the mixture to the saucepan and stir over low heat until the custard thickens and coats the back of a wooden spoon. Strain through a wire strainer.
Refrigerate, stirring from time to time until chilled.
Churn in an ice-cream maker.

CHOCOLATE SAUCE

6 oz bittersweet chocolate
3/4 cup milk
1/3 cup heavy cream
3 tablespoons granulated sugar
1 1/2 tablespoons unsalted butter, cut into small pieces

Place the chocolate in a heatproof bowl.
Bring the milk, cream, and sugar to a boil in a saucepan. Pour onto the chopped chocolate, whisking briskly to melt the chocolate.
Add the butter piece by piece and whisk until smooth.

TO SERVE

Put 2 scoops of ice cream into individual dishes or glass bowls, top with 2 pear halves and cover with hot chocolate sauce. Serve immediately.

Opera cakes

These square, iced chocolate cakes are proof that French patisserie is a form of alchemy: exact quantities, cooking times, and temperatures must be rigorously observed. Opera cakes, which can be frozen before they are frosted, are delicious with a glass of Cognac or a cup of coffee.

Makes 12 portions

GIOCONDA CAKE
1³/4 cups confectioners' sugar
2 cups almond flour
5 large eggs + 5 large egg whites
3 tablespoons unsalted butter
2 tablespoons granulated sugar
1/2 cup all-purpose flour

Preheat the oven to 450°F. Lightly butter the sides of 12 x 9 x 1 inch pans and line the bottoms with baking parchment.
Using an electric mixer, mix the confectioners' sugar, almond flour, and 3 of the eggs for 5 minutes, until thick. Add the 2 remaining eggs, one at a time, and beat for 5 minutes more.
Melt the butter in a saucepan, cool slightly, and whisk in a little of the batter. Beat the egg whites and granulated sugar until they form stiff peaks, and fold into the batter. Then fold in the flour and melted butter. Spread the mixture evenly in the prepared pans. Bake for 5–7 minutes, until the cake springs back when pressed in the center. Turn out onto wire racks, remove the paper, and cool completely.

COFFEE BUTTER CREAM
4 large egg yolks + 2 large egg whites
1¹/4 cups granulated sugar
1/2 cup milk
2 tablespoons cold water
3¹/2 sticks unsalted butter, at room temperature
1¹/2 tablespoons instant espresso dissolved in 2 tablespoons boiling water

Whisk the yolks in a heatproof bowl with 1/2 cup of the sugar. Bring the milk to a boil and whisk into the yolks. Return the mixture to the saucepan and stir over low heat until it thickens and coats the back of a wooden spoon. Strain through a wire strainer and cool.
Boil the remaining sugar and cold water to 250°F (hard-ball stage). Using an electric mixer, beat the egg whites until stiff peaks form, then carefully beat in the hot sugar syrup and continue to mix until the meringue is cool. Using clean beaters, beat the butter until smooth and then beat in the custard, espresso, and meringue, mixing until the butter cream is smooth.

COFFEE SYRUP
3/4 cup syrup (see recipe on page 30)
2 tablespoons instant espresso
2/3 cup boiling water

Dissolve the espresso in the boiling water. Add the syrup and cool.

TO ASSEMBLE THE CAKE
1 batch chocolate ganache (see recipe on page 8)
1 batch chocolate icing (see recipe on page 26)

Drizzle one-third of the coffee syrup over the first layer of cake and spread evenly with half the coffee butter cream. Cover with the second layer of cake, pressing down firmly without allowing the butter cream to ooze out. Drizzle with another portion of the coffee syrup, and spread this second layer with chocolate ganache. Cover with the third layer of cake, pressing as before. Drizzle with the remaining coffee syrup, and spread with the rest of the butter cream. Chill in the refrigerator for 3 hours.
With a rubber spatula, spread the icing evenly over the top surface of the cake. Set aside until the icing sets. Trim the sides with a sharp knife, and cut into portions.

Raspberry chocolate tart

Made with rich chocolate, sweet raspberries, smooth pastry cream and crunchy peanut brittle, this tart is a deliciously extravagant creation. If you prefer, you can make individual tartlets. A glass of port or strong red wine provides the perfect accompaniment to this after-dinner treat.

Serves 6

SWEET PASTRY
See page 8

Following the instructions on page 8, bake in an 8¹/₂-inch tart pan with a removable bottom. Cool completely.

PEANUT PRALINE
1 cup raw peanuts
³/₄ cup water
¹/₂ cup granulated sugar
pinch of salt

Preheat the oven to 375°F. Oil a rimmed baking sheet. Spread the peanuts in another baking pan and roast for 5–10 minutes, until golden.
Put the water and sugar in a pan and cook over medium heat, stirring continuously, until the syrup is caramel brown. Add the hot peanuts and salt, stirring well in so that the nuts are coated with caramel.
Turn out onto another oiled baking sheet and cool completely. Crush in a food processor into a fine powder.

CHOCOLATE PASTRY CREAM
3¹/₂ oz bittersweet chocolate, chopped
1¹/₄ cups pastry cream (see recipe on page 20)
¹/₄ cup heavy cream

Add the chocolate to the warm pastry cream. Let stand until the chocolate melts. Add the cream and whisk until smooth and creamy. Stir in the peanut praline.

TO ASSEMBLE THE TART
3 cups (12 oz) fresh raspberries
2-3 tablespoons peanut praline

Fill the baked pastry shell with the pastry cream. Cover with a tightly packed layer of raspberries. Serve the tart sprinkled with the peanut praline. The remaining peanut praline can be stored in an airtight container at room temperature for up to one month.

Chocolate savarins with vanilla cream

As is often the case in patisserie, the flavor of the vanilla in these savarins helps release the full aroma of the chocolate. Make the most of your vanilla by using a small knife to scrape out the seeds contained in the beans. In this recipe, the savarin sponge ring is drizzled with rum and covered with an apricot glaze, while the center is filled with vanilla cream.

Makes 1 savarin (8 servings)

VANILLA WHIPPED CREAM
2 cups heavy cream
1 vanilla bean, split open
1/4 cup granulated sugar

Chill the cream and the vanilla bean overnight. The next day, scrape the tiny seeds into the cream. Whip the cream with the sugar until firm peaks form. Chill overnight in the refrigerator.

CHOCOLATE SAVARIN MIXTURE
1/4 cup milk, heated to 105°-110°F
1(1/4 oz) envelope instant yeast
1³/4 cups all-purpose flour
3 tablespoons Dutch-processed cocoa powder
2 tablespoons granulated sugar
3 large eggs
1/8 teaspoon salt
5 tablespoons unsalted butter, melted and cooled
1/2 cup semisweet chocolate chips

Place the milk and yeast in the bowl of a heavy-duty electric mixer and stir to dissolve the yeast. Add the flour, cocoa, sugar, eggs, and salt, and stir well. Knead the dough rapidly for 5 minutes using the hook attachment. (Alternatively, mix in a bowl and knead well by hand.) Work the melted butter into the dough, then knead for 2 minutes more to make a soft, sticky dough. Mix in the chocolate chips. Cover and let rise until almost doubled, about 1¹/2 hours.
Grease a 9-inch savarin or ring mold. Fill it with the dough. Cover and let the dough rise until it just reaches the top of the mold, about 40 minutes.
Preheat the oven to 375°F. Bake about 20 minutes, until a wooden toothpick inserted into the dough comes out clean. Unmold onto a wire rack and cool slightly.

SAVARIN SYRUP
2 cups water
1¹/3 cups granulated sugar
1 vanilla bean, split open
1 3-inch cinnamon stick
1 star anise
1/2 orange, cut into wedges
1/2 lemon, cut into wedges
1/3 cup dark rum

While the savarin bakes, bring the water, sugar, vanilla bean, cinnamon, star anise, and orange and lemon wedges to a boil in a saucepan. Remove from the heat and let stand for 20 minutes. Strain through a wire strainer and stir in the rum.

TO ASSEMBLE THE SAVARINS
chocolate shavings
1/3 cup dark rum
1/2 cup apricot preserves, warmed

Place the warm savarin in a shallow dish and pour the warm syrup over the top. Baste the savarin often with the syrup until cooled. Drain on a wire rack, with a plate underneath to catch the drips, for 5 minutes. Drizzle the savarin with rum and brush with the warm preserves. Fill the savarin center with whipped cream rosettes, using a pastry bag with a 1/2-inch fluted tip. Decorate with chocolate shavings and chill in the refrigerator until ready to serve.

Chocolate mousse trilogy

Perfect for a dinner party, these mousses look as sensational as they taste. Served in individual glasses, the vibrant colors and flavors of the chocolate mousses and fruit coulis combine to create a feast for the eyes as well as the taste buds.

Serves 6

THREE FRUIT COULIS

ORANGE COULIS
1/2 teaspoon unflavored gelatin
1 tablespoon water
2/3 cup fresh orange juice, strained
3 tablespoons granulated sugar

PASSION FRUIT COULIS
1/2 teaspoon unflavored gelatin
1 tablespoon water
2/3 cup fresh strained or thawed frozen passion fruit purée (about 6 fruits, depending on size), plus extra for garnish
3 tablespoons granulated sugar

RASPBERRY COULIS
1/2 teaspoon unflavored gelatin
1 tablespoon water
1 cup fresh raspberry purée, plus a few whole raspberries for decoration
2 tablespoons granulated sugar

You'll need 18 small tequila glasses or tumblers (6 for each coulis).
For each coulis, sprinkle the gelatin over the water in 3 separate custard cups. Let stand about 3 minutes, until the gelatin is softened.
In separate small saucepans, stir the crushed fruit (or juice), sugar, and softened gelatin over low heat to dissolve the gelatin. Cool slightly. Divide each fruit coulis between 6 of the glasses while still warm. Refrigerate for 1 hour, or until set.

THREE CHOCOLATE MOUSSES

WHITE CHOCOLATE MOUSSE
3 1/2 oz white chocolate, melted and cooled to tepid
1 cup heavy cream

MILK CHOCOLATE MOUSSE
5 oz milk chocolate, melted and cooled to tepid
1 cup heavy cream

DARK CHOCOLATE MOUSSE
5 oz bittersweet chocolate, melted and cooled to tepid
1 cup heavy cream

Each of the three chocolate mousses is made in the same way. Using an electric mixer, whip the cream to a soft consistency—it shouldn't be too stiff. Add one-third of the whipped cream to the tepid chocolate and whisk to obtain a smooth, even texture. Fold in the remaining cream. Divide the chocolate cream mousses between the glasses containing the fruit coulis as follows:
• orange coulis and white chocolate mousse
• passion fruit coulis and milk chocolate mousse
• raspberry coulis and dark chocolate mousse
Chill in the refrigerator.

TO SERVE
18 pieces candied orange peel
passion fruit seeds
fresh raspberries
fresh mint leaves

Decorate each of the orange and white chocolate mousses with 3 pieces of candied orange peel; the passion fruit and milk chocolate mousses with a drizzle of passion fruit purée; and the raspberry and dark chocolate mousses with one or two raspberries and a mint leaf. Serve the chocolate mousse trilogies grouped together on individual rectangular dishes.

Chocolate ice cream duo

These ice creams are at their smoothest and creamiest if eaten as soon after churning as possible. Add chocolate shavings, roughly chopped cookies, or caramelized nuts, if you care to gild the lilies.

Each flavor makes about 1^1/$_2$ pints

DARK CHOCOLATE ICE CREAM
5 oz bittersweet chocolate, chopped
2 cups milk
^{1}/$_2$ cup heavy cream
^{2}/$_3$ cup granulated sugar
5 large egg yolks

MILK CHOCOLATE ICE CREAM
^{3}/$_4$ cup milk chocolate, chopped
2 cups milk
^{1}/$_2$ cup heavy cream
2 tablespoons granulated sugar
5 large egg yolks

FOR EACH FLAVOR
Place the chocolate in a heatproof bowl.
Bring the milk, cream, and half the sugar to a boil in a saucepan.
Whisk the egg yolks in a heatproof bowl with the remaining sugar until the mixture lightens in color, then whisk in the boiling milk.
Return the mixture to the saucepan and stir over low heat until it thickens and coats the back of a wooden spoon. Strain through a wire sieve over the chopped chocolate and whisk until all the chocolate has melted.
Refrigerate, stirring from time to time until chilled.
Churn each custard individually in an ice-cream maker.
Transfer to airtight containers and freeze for up to 3 days.

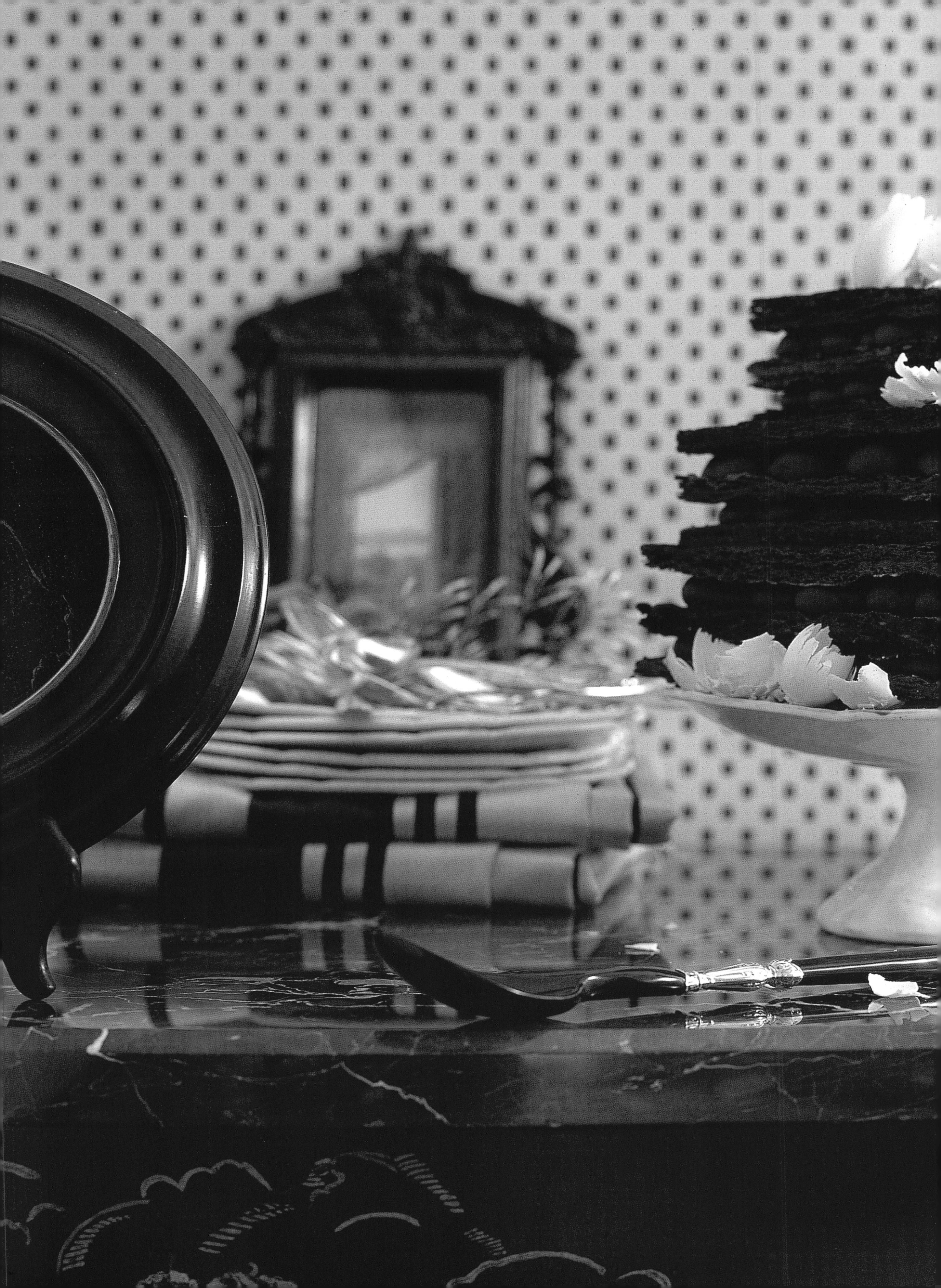

Pride

"Pride breakfasted with Plenty,
dined with Poverty, supped with Infamy."

—Benjamin Franklin

Chocolate orange tuiles

These crisp almond-flavored petit fours are delicious with coffee or ice cream. Their French name (*tuiles*) derives from the fact that they are shaped like curved roofing tiles. Keep them crisp by storing in an airtight container in a cool, dry place.

Makes about 30 cookies

1 cup chopped slivered almonds
2/3 cup granulated sugar
4 tablespoons (1/2 stick) unsalted butter, melted and cooled
2 large eggs, beaten
3 tablespoons Dutch-processed cocoa powder
1 1/2 tablespoons cornstarch
grated rind of 1 orange

Using a wooden spoon, mix all the ingredients together in a bowl until you have a smooth batter. Refrigerate for 1 hour.

Preheat the oven to 350°F. Line a baking sheet with baking parchment. It is best to bake these 1 sheet at a time for the best control of baking and cooling times. Using about 1 teaspoon for each cookie, spoon the batter about 4 inches apart on the sheet. Using the back of a spoon, spread the batter into 3 to 4-inch diameter rounds—they will be paper thin.

Bake until the cookies are set and no longer shiny, about 9 minutes. Remove from the oven and cool the cookies on the sheet just until they are firm enough to be lifted with a metal spatula, about 45 seconds. Drape the cookies over a rolling pin to cool and crisp into a curved shape. If the cookies cool and crisp and don't curve, return them to the oven to reheat and soften. Repeat with the remaining batter, using a cool baking sheet. Store in an airtight container in a cool, dry place.

Saint-Honoré

This classic French patisserie, named for the patron saint of pastry cooks, is thought to have been created by a pastrycook in the Rue Saint-Honoré in Paris. It takes skill to make and is best served the day it is made, when its light, creamy texture can be fully appreciated by the patient chef.

Serves 6

PLAIN PASTRY

1 cup all-purpose flour
pinch of salt
7 tablespoons (3/4 stick + 1 tablespoon) unsalted butter, chilled and cut into small pieces
1 large egg yolk, mixed with 2 tablespoons ice water

Mix the flour and salt in a bowl. Add the butter and rub with your fingertips until the mixture resembles coarse crumbs. Gradually stir in the yolk mixture, mixing just until the dough comes together (you may not need all of the mixture, or you may need to add a little ice water). Gather into a disk, wrap in plastic wrap, and refrigerate for at least 1 hour.
Roll out to a thickness of $1/8$ inch, and cut out a round 8 inches in diameter. Place on a baking sheet lined with baking parchment and prick all over with a fork. Chill in the refrigerator until ready to bake.

CHOUX PASTRY

$1/2$ cup milk
$1/2$ cup water
8 tablespoons (1 stick) unsalted butter, cut into small pieces
1 teaspoon sugar
$1/4$ teaspoon salt
1 cup all-purpose flour
4 large eggs

Bring the milk, water, butter, salt, and sugar to a boil in a saucepan. Add the flour all at once and stir with a wooden spoon for about 1 minute. Remove from the heat and mix in the eggs one at a time, stirring each one well in.
Preheat the oven to 400°F. Using a pastry bag with a $5/8$-inch tip, pipe two rings of warm choux pastry around the chilled pastry disk—the first $1/8$ inch from the edge and the second inside of the first. Pipe 15 small balls of choux pastry (about the size of a walnut) onto a separate baking sheet. Discard the remaining dough.
Bake separately until golden brown—20–25 minutes for the choux balls and 25–30 minutes for the base. Cool.

CHOCOLATE PASTRY CREAM

$1^1/4$ cups pastry cream (see recipe on page 20)
$2^1/4$ oz bittersweet chocolate, chopped
2 tablespoons heavy cream

Add the chocolate to the warm pastry cream. Let stand until the chocolate melts.
Add the heavy cream and whisk until smooth. Transfer to a pastry bag fitted with a fluted $1/4$-inch tip. Pierce the bottom of each ball and fill with the pastry cream. Working around the circumferences of the rings, pierce them with the tip and fill with the remaining pastry cream.

CARAMEL

$1/2$ cup sugar
2 tablespoons water

Boil the sugar and water, stirring constantly until it turns a pale caramel. Then plunge the base of the pan into cold water to stop cooking. Dip the top third of each choux ball into the caramel and place caramel-side up on a baking sheet lined with baking parchment. Let harden for 3–4 minutes, then arrange on the outer crown of choux pastry, using a little warmed caramel to hold in place.

DARK CHOCOLATE CREAM

$1^1/4$ cups heavy cream
5 oz bittersweet chocolate, melted and cooled to tepid

Using an electric mixer, whip the cream to soft peaks—not too stiff. Whisk one-third of the cream into the chocolate. Fold in the rest of the cream with a rubber spatula, stirring gently with a wooden spoon. Fill the center of the Saint-Honoré with two-thirds of the cream. Using a pastry bag with a fluted $1/2$-inch tip, decorate the top of the gateau with swirls of the remaining cream.

TO SERVE

Dutch-pressed cocoa powder
confectioners' sugar
chocolate shavings

Mix the cocoa and confectioners' sugar and sift over the Saint-Honoré. Sprinkle chocolate shavings in the center.

Profiteroles

The classic recipe for this rich dessert has been slightly varied by adding cocoa powder to the choux pastry. Don't forget to serve a little extra chocolate sauce to allow for extra indulgence!

Serves 8

CHOCOLATE CHOUX PASTRY

1/2 cup milk
1/2 cup water
8 tablespoons (1 stick) unsalted butter, cut into small pieces
1 teaspoon granulated sugar
1/4 teaspoon salt
1 cup all-purpose flour
2 tablespoons Dutch-processed cocoa powder
5 large eggs, 1 beaten
3 tablespoons finely chopped sliced almonds

Preheat the oven to 375°F.
Bring the milk, water, butter, sugar, and salt to a boil in a saucepan. Stir in the flour and cocoa with a wooden spoon for 1 minute. Remove from the heat and add the 4 eggs one at a time, stirring each one well in.
Using a pastry bag with a 1/2-inch tip, pipe 24 small balls of choux pastry (about the size of a walnut) onto a baking sheet. Discard the remaining pastry.
Lightly brush the balls with beaten egg. Sprinkle with chopped almonds. Bake for 20–25 minutes, until puffed and crisp. Cool completely.

VANILLA ICE CREAM

2 cups milk
3/4 cup heavy cream
3/4 cup granulated sugar
2 vanilla beans, split open
7 large egg yolks

Bring the milk, cream, half the sugar, and the vanilla beans to a boil in a saucepan. Remove from the heat and let stand for 20 minutes.
Whisk the egg yolks with the rest of the sugar until the mixture lightens in color.
Remove the vanilla beans from the milk. Whisk the milk into the egg yolks.
Return the mixture to the saucepan and cook over low heat until it thickens and coats the back of a wooden spoon, then strain through a wire strainer.
Chill in the refrigerator, stirring from time to time.
Churn in an ice-cream maker.

CHOCOLATE SAUCE

4 oz bittersweet chocolate, chopped
1/2 cup milk
1/4 cup heavy cream
2 tablespoons granulated sugar
2 teaspoons unsalted butter, cut into small pieces

Place the chocolate in a heatproof bowl.
Bring the milk, cream, and sugar to a boil in a saucepan. Pour onto the chopped chocolate and let stand to melt the chocolate. Add the butter and whisk until smooth.

TO ASSEMBLE THE PROFITEROLES

confectioners' sugar

Cut each profiterole in half. Fill the bottom half with a small scoop of vanilla ice cream and cover with the top half. Sprinkle with sugar. Quickly arrange the profiteroles in individual dishes or on a serving dish, drizzle with hot chocolate sauce, and serve immediately.

Twelfth-Night cake

Galette des Rois, or "King's Cakes," are eaten in France to celebrate Epiphany. The tradition is thought to date from Roman times when a festival held on the winter solstice offered everyone—freedmen and slaves alike—an opportunity to be king for a day if their portion of cake contained a small lucky charm. The creation of this cake, especially the puff pastry, requires a certain degree of skill during the rolling and folding process. For the best results, start making the pastry the day before, rolling and folding the mixture four times, and finish the next day, rolling and folding twice. The chocolate version of the cake goes particularly well with raspberries and champagne—a truly royal finish.

Serves 6

CHOCOLATE PUFF PASTRY

FOR THE DOUGH
1³/4 cups all-purpose flour
²/₃ cup water
2 tablespoons unsalted butter, melted
³/4 teaspoon salt

FOR THE TOURAGE
18 tablespoons (2¹/4 sticks) unsalted butter, at room temperature
2 tablespoons confectioners' sugar
3 tablespoons Dutch-processed cocoa powder

To make the dough, mix the flour, water, melted butter, and salt. Shape into a flat, thick square, wrap with plastic wrap, and chill for 1 hour.
For the tourage, cream the butter with a rubber spatula, then work in the sugar and cocoa. Shape into a 6-inch square, wrap with plastic wrap and chill about 1 hour, until it is cool but malleable.
Flour the work surface and roll out the dough into an 8-inch square. Place the butter square, with 2 corners pointing north and south, in the center of the square dough. Fold over the corners of the dough to cover the butter, and pinch closed. Roll the dough into a rectangle, 20 inches by 8 inches. Fold one-third down and the other third up over that, brushing off excess flour. Turn the pastry vertically and, with the rolling pin at right angles, process once again. Chill for 30 minutes.
Repeat the roll and fold sequences four more times, making sure you chill the pastry in the refrigerator for at least 30 minutes between each roll. Altogether, the pastry should be rolled and folded 6 times.

GLAZE
2 large egg yolks
1 tablespoon milk
pinch of salt

Whisk all the ingredients together.

CHOCOLATE FRANGIPANE
6 tablespoons (³/4 stick) unsalted butter, at room temperature
¹/2 cup almond flour
3 tablespoons granulated sugar
1 large egg yolk, beaten
1 tablespoon cornstarch
1 tablespoon dark rum
2 oz bittersweet chocolate, chopped

Beat the butter with an electric mixer on high speed until fluffy. Add the almond flour, sugar, and beaten egg, and mix well. Then stir in the cornstarch and rum. Melt the chocolate in a microwave or in a bowl set over a pan of barely simmering water, add to the almond mixture, and mix well.

TO ASSEMBLE AND BAKE THE CAKE
3 tablespoons raspberry preserves (not seedless)
1 "lucky charm," wrapped in baking parchment
Glaze (see recipe on the left), as needed

Divide the pastry in two and roll out each half to a thickness of ¹/8 inch. Cut two rounds, each 10¹/2 inches in diameter, and place one on a baking sheet lined with baking parchment. Spread evenly with the raspberry preserves, leaving a ³/4-inch border around the edge.
Top with the frangipane and bury the charm (always pre-warn unsuspecting guests!). Brush the pastry border with glaze and place the second round on top of the first. Then press the edges firmly together so that they are well sealed. Brush the top with the glaze and crimp the edges. Chill in the refrigerator for 1 hour.
Preheat the oven to 375°F. Glaze again. Using a small knife, score a pattern of curved lines from the center to the edges. Bake for 40–45 minutes, until puffed and crisp. Cool on the baking sheet.

Chocolate macaroons

These small sandwiched cookies, crunchy on the outside and deliciously soft on the inside, have been baked in Europe for hundreds of years. The recipe originated in Italy during the Renaissance (the name derives from the Italian *maccherone* and the Venetian *macarone*, meaning "fine paste"). The most popular filling is the traditional chocolate ganache, though it can be replaced by a number of other fillings, such as chocolate banana jam or raspberry jam.

Makes about 36 cookies

MACAROONS

1 1/4 cups confectioners' sugar
1 cup almond flour
5 tablespoons Dutch-processed cocoa powder
3 large egg whites, at room temperature
1/4 cup granulated sugar

Process the confectioners' sugar, almond flour, and cocoa in a food processor until ground to an extremely fine powder.
Using an electric mixer, beat the egg whites and granulated sugar until they form stiff peaks. Carefully fold in the cocoa mixture with a rubber spatula, mixing downward to the center of the bowl, then up to the edges and back toward the center, until you obtain a smooth, even texture.
Using a pastry bag fitted with a 1/2-inch plain tip, pipe 3/4-inch wide mounds of the macaroon mixture onto a baking sheet lined with baking parchment. Let stand at room temperature for 30 minutes, until a thin film forms on the mounds.
Preheat the oven to 350°. Bake the macaroons for about 15 minutes, until the edges of the macaroons are firm and crisp. Cool 5 minutes, then transfer to a wire rack and cool completely.

CHOCOLATE GANACHE

4 oz bittersweet chocolate, chopped
1/3 cup heavy cream

Place the chocolate in a heatproof bowl.
Pour the cream into a pan, bring to a boil, and pour onto the chopped chocolate. Let stand until the chocolate is melted. Whisk until the ganache is smooth and shiny. Cool until the ganache is thick enough to spread.

TO ASSEMBLE THE MACAROONS

Stick the macaroons together in pairs with chocolate ganache. Refrigerate until ready to serve.

Kouglofs

Traditionally eaten at Sunday breakfast, these yeast cakes are made with raisins and are a regional specialty of Alsace, though Germany, Austria, and Poland also claim credit for them. There are special molds for these cakes, but terracotta ones give the most evenly distributed heat and authentic flavor.

Makes 2 x 7-inch cakes

1/2 cup raisins
1 tablespoon dark rum
2 1/2 cups all-purpose flour
3 1/2 tablespoons Dutch-processed cocoa powder
2/3 cup + 2 tablespoons granulated sugar
2/3 cup milk
1 large egg + 1 large egg yolk
1 (1/4-oz) package instant yeast
1/4 teaspoon salt
10 tablespoons (1 1/4 sticks) unsalted butter, at room temperature, cut into small pieces, plus 4 tablespoons (1/2 stick) unsalted butter, melted
1/3 cup semisweet chocolate chips
3 tablespoons sliced almonds
1 teaspoon ground cinnamon

Soak the raisins in the rum.
Stir the flour, cocoa, 2 tablespoons of sugar, milk, egg, egg yolk, yeast, and salt in the bowl of a heavy-duty electric mixer. Using the dough hook, starting at low speed and gradually building up to moderate, knead for about 10 minutes or until the mixture is elastic and smooth. (Alternatively, mix well in a bowl and knead by hand.)
Add the softened butter, 1 tablespoon at a time, until the butter is thoroughly worked into the dough. Then add the soaked raisins and chocolate chips. Cover the bowl and let rise at room temperature for 30 minutes, until doubled in volume.

Butter two 7-inch kouglof molds or deep ring molds, and sprinkle the insides with the almonds.
Knead the air out of the dough and divide in half. On a floured work surface, roll and form one of the pieces of dough into a log with floured hands. Place the dough in the base of the mold. Repeat the process with the other half of the dough and place in the second mold. Cover and let rise for about 1 hour at room temperature—the dough should rise almost to the top of the molds.
Preheat the oven to 375°F. Bake for 40–45 minutes, until golden brown. Turn the cakes out of the mold and cool on a wire rack. Brush the melted butter over the kouglofs. Mix the remaining 2/3 cup sugar with the cinnamon, and sprinkle over the kouglofs.

Concorde

This delicious dessert consists of alternate layers of meringue and chocolate mousse, and is famously light and frothy. The meringue, which you may prefer plain (substitute additional confectioners' sugar for one cocoa, and mix in half a teaspoon of vanilla at the end of making the meringue), can be prepared in advance, provided it is kept dry in an airtight container.

Serves 6

CHOCOLATE MERINGUE
4 large egg whites
1/2 cup granulated sugar
1 cup confectioners' sugar
31/2 tablespoons Dutch-processed cocoa powder

Using an electric mixer, beat the egg whites until they form stiff peaks, adding the granulated sugar about halfway through. Sift the confectioners' sugar and cocoa together and fold thoroughly into the egg whites. Preheat the oven to 275°F. Using a pastry bag with a 1/2-inch plain tip, pipe two disks of meringue (6 inches in diameter) onto 1 baking sheet lined with baking parchment. Change to an 1/8-inch tip and pipe the rest of the meringue into thin 3-inch long strips on another parchment-lined baking sheet, making sure they are spaced one inch apart. Pipe more strips on the sheet with the disks.
Bake for 11/2 hours, until the meringue is dry and brittle. Cool on the baking sheets.

CHOCOLATE MOUSSE
2 large egg yolks
2 tablespoons granulated sugar
1/3 cup milk
1/3 cup heavy cream
7 oz bittersweet chocolate, chopped
11/4 cup heavy cream

Whisk the yolks and sugar in a heatproof bowl until the mixture lightens in color. Bring the milk and cream to a boil in a saucepan. Whisk into the egg mixture. Return the mixture to the saucepan and stir over low heat until it thickens and coats the back of a wooden spoon. Strain through a wire strainer into a heatproof bowl.
Add the chocolate to the hot crème anglaise. Let stand to melt the chocolate, then whisk until smooth. Cool to room temperature, stirring often. Using an electric mixer, beat the cream to a soft consistency—it should not be too stiff. Whisk one-third of the whipped cream into the cool chocolate and custard mixture, then fold in the rest of the cream.

TO ASSEMBLE THE CONCORDE
Dutch-processed cocoa powder

Place one of the meringue disks in a springform pan, 7 inches in diameter and 3 inches deep. Reserve 1/3 cup of the mousse, cover and refrigerate. Cover the disk with half of the remaining chocolate mousse. Add the second meringue disk and the remaining mousse. Refrigerate for 4 hours, until the mousse is firm.
To serve, remove the ring. Cut the meringue sticks into pieces, about 3/4 inch long. Spread the reserved mousse in a thin layer on the sides of the cake. Press the sticks onto the top and sides of the cake to cover it completely. Dust with cocoa powder. Refrigerate until serving.

Mille-feuille

Known to American bakers as a chocolate napoleon, in France this popular dessert is always called "Mille-feuille," meaning "thousand leaves." Under either name, the rich chocolate is the perfect complement to the smoothness of the pastry cream and the lightness of the puff pastry. To make sure the pastry remains crisp, don't add the filling until the last minute—adding the pastry cream too early will detract from the crisp, light texture of the mille-feuille.

Serves 6-8

CHOCOLATE PUFF PASTRY
see page 62

Cut the chilled pastry into thirds. Roll out each piece 1/8-inch thick, and trim into an 8 1/2-inch square. Place each piece on a baking sheet lined with baking parchment and prick all over with a fork. Chill in the refrigerator for 1 hour.
Preheat the oven to 400°F. Bake the pastry squares for about 20 minutes, until puffed and crisp. Cool on the baking sheets.

CHOCOLATE PASTRY CREAM
4 oz bittersweet chocolate, melted
1 double batch pastry cream (see recipe on page 20)
1/4 cup heavy cream

Add the chocolate to the warm pastry cream. Let stand to melt the chocolate. Add the cream, and whisk well until smooth and creamy.

TO ASSEMBLE THE MILLE-FEUILLE
confectioners' sugar
Dutch-processed cocoa powder
bittersweet chocolate shavings

Using a pastry bag with a smooth 1/2-inch tip, pipe half the pastry cream in balls onto the first layer. Cover with a second layer of mille-feuille and pipe on the rest of the pastry cream. Top with the third layer of pastry, placing the smoothest side uppermost.
Decorate the top of the mille-feuille by dividing it diagonally with a piece of parchment paper. Sift confectioners' sugar over one half, and cocoa powder over the other half. Scatter a few chocolate shavings in the center. Use a serrated knife to cut into portions.

Envy

"Envy is one of the classic deadly sins that prevents us from truly rejoicing in the good fortune of others."

—La Rochefoucauld

Madeleines

The origin of these small tea cakes is the subject of much debate. According to one theory, they were created—and named after—a young peasant girl in the French region of Lorraine, who was noticed by the wife of Louis XV. Some years later, madeleines were immortalized by the French writer, Marcel Proust, who described how a piece of this "seashell cake so strictly pleated on the outside and so sensual inside" caused childhood memories to come flooding back (*Remembrance of Things Past*). Today, baking madeleines is much easier since the modern nonstick versions of the ribbed oval molds that given them their rounded, shell-like appearance do not need to be buttered or floured.

Makes approximately 30 madeleines

1 cup + 2 tablespoons (2 1/4 sticks) unsalted butter
3 large eggs, at room temperature
3/4 cup granulated sugar
2 tablespoons wildflower honey
1/3 cup tablespoons milk
1 3/4 cups all-purpose flour
2 teaspoons baking powder
3 tablespoons Dutch-processed cocoa powder
1 oz bittersweet chocolate, melted and cooled to tepid

Prepare the madeleine batter 24 hours in advance. Heat butter in a pan until it turns a light nut-brown color. Set aside to cool to lukewarm. Beat the eggs, sugar, honey, and milk with an electric mixer until well combined. Sift together the flour, cocoa, and baking powder. Add to the egg mixture and stir well. Mix in the warm butter and melted chocolate. Cover and refrigerate for 24 hours. The next day, preheat the oven to 425°F. Lightly butter and flour the madeleine molds (unless they are the nonstick variety). Spoon about 1 tablespoon of the batter into each mold. Bake until the madeleines have formed their distinctive hump and are lightly browned, about 10 minutes. Unmold onto a wire cake rack and cool completely.

Temptation

Sophisticated—and aptly named—this creation will add elegance to any dinner party. Although it requires a certain degree of skill, it is possible to simplify things at the frosting stage. Instead of icing the cake—always a fairly delicate operation—you can simply dust it with Dutch-processed cocoa powder and decorate with chopped pistachio nuts. This is a dessert for those extra special occasions—the chocolate-brownie layer is covered with pistachio cream and then the whole cake coated with a layer of chocolate mousse.

Serves 6

CHOCOLATE-BROWNIE LAYER
1 oz bittersweet chocolate, chopped
4 tablespoons (1/2 stick) unsalted butter, at room temperature
1 large egg
2 tablespoons granulated sugar
2 tablespoons light brown sugar
1/4 cup all-purpose flour
1/3 cup chopped walnuts

Preheat the oven to 350°F. Melt the chocolate in a heatproof bowl set over a pan of barely simmering water. Add the butter and whisk until smooth. Whisk in the egg, and the granulated and brown sugars. Stir in the flour, then the walnuts. Spread the batter in a lightly buttered 6-inch cake pan with a removable bottom. Bake until the cake springs back when pressed in the center, about 15 minutes. Cool completely in the pan on a wire cake rack.

PISTACHIO CREAM
1 teaspoon powdered gelatin
1 tablespoon water
4 large egg yolks
1/4 cup granulated sugar
1 cup heavy cream
1/4 cup pistachio paste

Sprinkle the gelatin over the water in a custard cup and let stand 5 minutes. Whisk the yolks and sugar in a heatproof bowl until the mixture lightens in color. Bring the cream to a boil and whisk into the yolk mixture. Return the mixture to the saucepan and add the soaked gelatin. Stir over low heat until it thickens and coats the back of a wooden spoon. Whisk in the pistachio paste.
Strain through a wire sieve into a bowl. Refrigerate until partially set. Pour over the cake in the pan and smooth the top. Freeze until the cream is firm, about 2 hours.

CHOCOLATE MOUSSE
3 tablespoons sugar
2 tablespoons water
3 large egg yolks
4 oz bittersweet chocolate, melted and cooled to tepid
3/4 cup heavy cream

Bring the sugar and water to a full boil. Beating the yolks with an electric mixer, pour the hot syrup into the yolks, and beat until the yolks are cool and doubled in volume. Using clean beaters, whip the cream until light and fluffy, but not too stiff. Whisk one-third of the whipped cream into the tepid chocolate. Then, using a rubber spatula, fold in the yolk mixture, then the remaining cream. Spread the mousse over the pistachio layer (enjoy leftover mousse as the cook's treat). Cover and freeze until firm, at least 4 hours.

TO ASSEMBLE THE CAKE
Chocolate icing (see recipe in recipe booklet, page 5)
10 small chocolate macaroons (see recipe on page 64), optional
2 tablespoons finely chopped pistachios

Run a hot wet knife around the inside of the cake pan and remove the sides. Place the cake on a wire cake rack on a baking sheet. Quickly pour all of the tepid, but fluid icing over the cake and immediately smooth it over the top, letting the excess run down the sides; smooth as needed. Decorate with halved macaroons if using, and sprinkle with chopped pistachios. Freeze to set the icing. Freeze for up to 3 days. Thaw for 8 hours in the refrigerator before serving.

Chocolate and salted-caramel tart

A study in contrasts, this tart combines sweet pastry with salted-caramel cream, and is topped with dark chocolate Chantilly and hazelnut crunch. The crunchiness of the sea salt and hazelnuts, the frothiness of the Chantilly, and the smoothness of the caramel cream offer a delightful contrast of textures and flavors. When baking, remember to make a dark caramel, as it is not quite as sweet and has a much richer flavor. If you prefer, you can make individual tartlets rather than a large tart.

Serves 6

SWEET PASTRY
see page 8

Bake the pastry in a 9-inch tart pan with a removable bottom as directed on page 8. Cool completely.

HAZELNUT BRITTLE
1/2 cup granulated sugar
8 tablespoons (1 stick) unsalted butter, thinly sliced
3/4 cup toasted, peeled, and coarsely chopped hazelnuts
pinch of sea salt

Lightly oil a metal spatula and rimmed baking sheet and place the sheet on a heatproof surface. Cook the sugar and butter in a saucepan over high heat, stirring constantly, until a candy thermometer reads 310°F, about 10 minutes. Add the hazelnuts and salt and swirl the pan to mix. Pour onto the baking sheet and spread thinly with the spatula. Cool completely.

SALTED-CARAMEL CREAM
1 teaspoon powdered gelatin
1 tablespoon water
1 cup heavy cream
1/2 cup sugar
4 large egg yolks
4 tablespoons (1/2 stick) unsalted butter, cut into small pieces
1/8 teaspoon sea salt, preferably fleur de sel

Sprinkle the gelatin over the water in a custard cup and let stand for 5 minutes. Bring the cream to a boil and set aside. Put the sugar in a separate, tall saucepan without any liquid and cook over high heat, stirring continuously with a wooden spoon, until melted and dark caramel in color. Carefully whisk in the hot cream (it will boil up) and cook until the caramel is dissolved.

Whisk the yolks in a heatproof bowl and whisk in the caramel mixture. Return the mixture to the saucepan and add the soaked gelatin. Stir over low heat until it thickens and coats the back of a wooden spoon. Remove from the heat and stir in the butter and sea salt. Strain through a wire sieve into a bowl and refrigerate until beginning to set. Spread in the baked pastry shell and refrigerate until chilled fully set.

DARK CHOCOLATE WHIPPED CREAM
3/4 cup heavy cream
31/2 oz bittersweet chocolate, melted and cooled to tepid

Whip the cream using an electric mixer until soft peaks form—it should not be too stiff. Whisk one-third of the whipped cream into the tepid chocolate until smooth. Fold in the remaining whipped cream with a rubber spatula. Using a piping bag with a fluted 1/2 inch tip, cover the surface of the tart with whipped cream rosettes.

TO SERVE
Break the hazelnut brittle into 11/4 -11/2 inch shards and dot the surface of the tart at irregular intervals. Remove the tart from the pan.

White-chocolate blondies with raspberries

In this original twist on the traditional chocolate brownie recipe, the sweetness of the white chocolate and fruity flavor of the raspberries is refreshing—and slightly unexpected.

Makes 20 blondies

6 oz white chocolate, chopped
1 cup plus 6 tablespoons (2³/4 sticks) unsalted butter, at room temperature
5 large eggs
1³/4 cups granulated sugar
1 cup chopped natural almonds
1³/4 cups all-purpose flour
1 cup fresh raspberries
2 tablespoons confectioners' sugar

Preheat the oven to 350°F.

Melt the chocolate in a heatproof bowl set over a pan of barely simmering water (the bowl must not touch the water). With the bowl still over the water, add the butter and whisk until smooth. Whisk in the eggs, one at a time, and then the sugar. Remove the bowl from the saucepan. Stir in the flour until combined. Mix in the almonds.

Butter the sides of a rectangular baking pan—13 inches long by 9 inches wide and 1 inch deep—and line the bottom with baking parchment. Spread the batter in the pan and sprinkle with the raspberries. (You can vary the shape of the blondies by using differently shaped cake pans and molds. For the round blondies in the photograph, spoon the batter into unlined, globe-shaped silicone molds with 3¹/4 inch diameters.)

Bake until golden brown and a wooden toothpick inserted in the center comes out clean, about 25 minutes (less if making the round blondies). Cool in the pan on a wire cake rack. Invert to unmold the entire blondie, peel off the paper, and cut into 20 pieces. Garnish with a light sprinkling of confectioners' sugar.

Truffles

In France, these intense chocolates are traditionally given at Christmas, though they can be enjoyed at any time of year. You can flavor the truffles by infusing the cream with cinnamon (3 sticks), Earl Grey tea (2–3 teabags), or vanilla (2 beans).

Makes about 40 truffles

12 oz bittersweet chocolate, chopped
3/4 cup heavy cream
3 tablespoons unsalted butter, cut into small pieces
3/4 cup Dutch-processed cocoa powder
1/2 cup confectioners' sugar (optional)

Melt the chocolate in a heatproof bowl set over a pan of barely simmering water (the bowl must not touch the water). Keep warm. Bring the cream to a boil. Pour over the chocolate and whisk until combined. Add the butter and whisk until the butter is absorbed. Spread the mixture evenly in an 8-inch square dish lined on the bottom and two opposite sides with a single piece of baking parchment. Refrigerate until firm, at least 8 hours.

The next day, lift up on the paper to remove the truffle mixture from the dish. Cut into pieces about 3/4 inch square, then roll them into balls. Place the cocoa powder in a shallow dish and roll the truffles in the cocoa to coat them. Some can be rolled in confectioners' sugar for a contrast, if desired. Refrigerate until firm again.

Chocolate mousse

This dessert has a number of points in its favor: it is easy to make, it can be prepared the day before, and it makes the perfect light finish to any meal. This classic version can easily be given extra flavor by adding orange rind or pieces of candied orange peel. You can also flavor the cream by infusing it with spices.

Serves 6

9 oz bittersweet chocolate, chopped
1/2 cup heavy cream
6 large egg whites, at room temperature
3 tablespoons granulated sugar
chocolate shavings, for garnish

Melt the chocolate in a heatproof bowl set over a pan of barely simmering water (the bowl must not touch the water). Cool until tepid but still fluid.
Bring the cream to a boil. Pour over melted chocolate and whisk until smooth. Beat the egg whites with the sugar until stiff peaks form. Whisk about one-fourth of the beaten egg whites into the chocolate mixture. Gently fold in the remaining egg whites with a rubber spatula until the mousse is evenly colored.
Transfer the mousse to a serving dish or spoon into individual glasses. Refrigerate until chilled, at least 3 hours. Just before serving, decorate the mousse with the chocolate shavings.

Paris-Brest

In 1891, a Parisian pastrycook named his latest creation after the famed bicycle race between Paris and Brest. This ring-shaped cake, reminiscent of a bicycle wheel, is traditionally made from choux pastry, filled with praline-flavored cream, and sprinkled with slivered almonds. This version, filled with chocolate butter cream, works just as well, especially when served warm.

Serves 6

CHOUX PASTRY

1/4 cup slivered almonds
1/2 cup milk
1/2 cup water
8 tablespoons (1 stick) unsalted butter, cut into small pieces
pinch of salt
1 teaspoon sugar
1 cup all-purpose flour
4 large eggs, at room temperature
1 large egg yolk mixed with 1 tablespoon milk
2 tablespoons pearl sugar or sanding sugar

Preheat the oven to 375°F.
Spread the almonds on a baking sheet and bake until golden, about 10 minutes. Cool completely.
Mix the milk, water, butter, salt, and sugar together in a pan and bring to a boil. Add all of the flour and stir over low heat with a wooden spoon until smooth and thick, about 1 minute. Remove from the heat. One at a time, stir in the eggs, beating well between additions.
Using a pastry bag with a plain 11/16-inch tip, pipe a ring of pastry, 7 inches in diameter, onto a baking sheet lined with baking parchment. Pipe a second ring immediately inside the first. Pipe a third ring on top of the other two, along the line of the join. Discard the remaining pastry.
Lightly brush the rings with some of the egg yolk mixture. Sprinkle with the toasted almonds and pearl sugar.
Bake until puffed, golden brown, and crisp, about 30 minutes. Do not open the door during the first 20 minutes. Remove from the oven and cool completely on the baking sheet.

CHOCOLATE BUTTER CREAM

2 oz bittersweet chocolate, melted
11/4 cups pastry cream (see recipe on page 20)
10 tablespoons (11/4 sticks) unsalted butter, at room temperature

Add the chocolate to the warm pastry cream and let stand until the chocolate melts. Whisk until smooth. Cool until tepid.
Beat the butter in the bowl of a heavy-duty electric mixer with the whisk attachment until smooth and creamy. Gradually beat in the chocolate pastry cream until the butter cream is smooth.

TO ASSEMBLE THE PARIS-BREST

confectioners' sugar

Cut the pastry ring in half horizontally using a serrated knife. Using a pastry bag with a 1/2-inch fluted tip, pipe swirls of chocolate butter cream onto base.
Replace the top, pressing down gently to make a good contact, but not so that the filling oozes out. Dust with the confectioners' sugar.

Avarice

"Avarice has ruined more
souls than extravagance"

—Charles Caleb Colton

Chocolate goblets

Contrasting textures and temperatures unite in this dessert. First, the goblets are lined with chocolate ganache sprinkled with chocolate cookie crumbs. Then comes the melting texture of the chocolate sorbet and a delicate coating of chocolate sauce interspersed with more crumbs (you don't need to dip the goblets in chocolate as shown in the picture opposite, except for decorative purposes of course!)

Makes 6 goblets

CHOCOLATE SORBET
4 oz bittersweet chocolate, chopped
1/3 cup plus 1 tablespoon Dutch-processed cocoa powder
1 1/4 cups water
1/2 cup granulated sugar

Place the chocolate in a heatproof bowl with the cocoa. Bring the water and sugar to a rolling boil in a saucepan. Pour the syrup over the chocolate and cocoa and whisk to melt the chocolate. Refrigerate until chilled. Churn in an ice cream maker. Store in the freezer.

CHOCOLATE CRUMBS
2/3 cup all-purpose flour
4 tablespoons (1/2 stick) unsalted butter, at room temperature
3 tablespoons light brown sugar
1 tablespoon Dutch-processed cocoa powder
1 tablespoon semisweet chocolate chips
pinch of salt
pinch of ground cinnamon

Preheat the oven to 350°F.
Rub all of the ingredients together in a mixing bowl with your fingertips until the mixture is coarse and crumbly. Refrigerate for 1 hour.
Spread the mixture evenly on a baking sheet lined with baking parchment.
Bake until the crumbs are firm, 15–20 minutes. Remove from the oven and cool.

CREAMY CHOCOLATE GANACHE
5 oz bittersweet chocolate, chopped
3/4 cup heavy cream
3/4 cup milk
5 large egg yolks
3 tablespoons sugar

Place the chocolate in a heatproof bowl. Bring the cream and milk to a boil in a saucepan. Whisk the yolks and sugar in another heatproof bowl until the mixture lightens, then whisk in the boiling milk mixture. Return the mixture to the saucepan and stir over low heat until it thickens and coats the back of a wooden spoon. Strain over the chopped chocolate and whisk until all the chocolate has melted.
Spread equal amounts of the ganache on the insides of 6 glass goblets. Refrigerate, swirling the goblets occasionally to create a thick coating of ganache, until the ganache is set but still tacky, about 3 hours.

DARK CHOCOLATE SAUCE
5 oz bittersweet chocolate, chopped
1/3 cup milk
1/4 cup heavy cream
2 tablespoons sugar
2 teaspoons unsalted butter

Place the chocolate in a heatproof bowl. Bring the milk, cream, and sugar to a boil in a saucepan. Pour over the chopped chocolate and whisk until the chocolate is melted. Add the butter and whisk until smooth and shiny.

TO ASSEMBLE THE GOBLETS
chocolate shavings

Lightly crush the crumbs and sprinkle a few pieces on the ganache in the goblets. Add a scoop of the sorbet and then top with the warm chocolate sauce. To finish, sprinkle with a few chocolate shavings and more crumbs. Serve immediately.

Liégeois

Café liégeois is a classic iced coffee dessert, both elegant and extravagant. In this chocolate version, the chilled chocolate milk and chocolate ice cream offer a delicious contrast to the warm chocolate sauce and melting vanilla-flavored whipped cream, resulting in a dessert that will appeal to chocolate lovers of all ages.

Serves 6

DARK CHOCOLATE ICE CREAM
5 oz bittersweet chocolate, chopped
2 cups milk
1/2 cup heavy cream
2/3 cup granulated sugar
5 large egg yolks

Place the chocolate in a heatproof bowl.
Bring the milk, cream, and 1/3 cup sugar into a saucepan and bring to a boil. Whisk the yolks with the remaining 1/3 cup sugar in a heatproof bowl until the mixture lightens, then whisk in the boiling milk mixture. Return the mixture to the saucepan and stir over low heat until it thickens and coats the back of a wooden spoon.
Strain through a wire sieve into the chopped chocolate and whisk until the chocolate has completely melted. Refrigerate until chilled, stirring from time to time. Churn in an ice-cream maker.

CHOCOLATE MILK
3 oz bittersweet chocolate, chopped
1 cup milk
1/4 cup heavy cream
1 tablespoon light brown sugar

Place the chocolate in a heatproof bowl. Bring the milk and cream to a boil in a saucepan. Pour the mixture carefully over the chopped chocolate and whisk until smooth. Stir in the brown sugar and refrigerate until chilled.

DARK CHOCOLATE SAUCE
5 oz bittersweet chocolate, chopped
1/3 cup milk
1/4 cup heavy cream
2 tablespoons granulated sugar
2 teaspoons unsalted butter

Place the chocolate in a heatproof bowl.
Bring the milk, cream, and granulated sugar to a boil in a saucepan. Pour over the chopped chocolate and whisk until the chocolate is melted. Add the butter and whisk until smooth and shiny.

VANILLA WHIPPED CREAM
1 vanilla bean
1 1/4 cups heavy cream
1/4 cup confectioners' sugar

Split open the vanilla bean and scrape out the seeds with the point of a knife. Put the cream, confectioners' sugar, and vanilla seeds in a mixing bowl. Beat with an electric mixer until light and fluffy.

TO ASSEMBLE THE LIÉGEOIS
Dutch-processed cocoa powder

Divide the chocolate milk between 6 tall glasses. Add 2 scoops of chocolate ice cream to each glass. Cover with warm chocolate sauce and top with the vanilla whipped cream. Garnish with a sprinkling of cocoa powder. Serve immediately.

Chocolate and poached-pear tart

Served warm, this elegant dessert combines the complementary flavors of chocolate, rich wine, spices, and fresh fruit. A light, red Beaujolais (for example, Brouilly or, in season, a Beaujolais Nouveau) makes an ideal accompaniment.

Serves 6

PEARS POACHED IN WINE

3 firm-ripe pears, such as D'anjou
1³/4 cups light red wine, such as Beaujolais
³/4 cup granulated sugar
1 cinnamon stick
1 vanilla bean, split open
1 star anise

Peel and halve the pears lengthwise, and remove the core. Bring the wine, sugar, cinnamon, vanilla, and star anise to a boil in a saucepan. Add the pears to the wine and simmer over low heat, just until tender when pierced with the tip of a small knife, about 15 minutes. Do not overcook. Refrigerate overnight in the wine syrup.

SWEET PASTRY

See page 8

Line a 9-inch tart pan with a removable bottom with the pastry. Bake and cool as directed on page 8.

CHOCOLATE-RED WINE GANACHE

5 oz bittersweet chocolate, chopped
¹/2 cup heavy cream
3 tablespoons unsalted butter, cut into small pieces
3 tablespoons light red wine, such as Beaujolais

Place the chocolate in a heatproof bowl.
Bring the cream to a boil, pour over chopped chocolate and whisk until the chocolate has completely melted. Whisk in the butter, a piece at a time, and then whisk in the wine until the ganache is smooth.
Pour the ganache into the baked tart shell and refrigerate until barely set, about 30 minutes.

TO ASSEMBLE THE TART

confectioners' sugar
chocolate shavings

Drain and then thinly slice the pears. Arrange them in concentric circles on the ganache. Dust the edges of the tart with sugar and garnish with chocolate shavings in the center. Remove the tart from the pan. If you prefer, make 6 individual tarts rather than 1 large tart.

Fruited chocolate muffins

These muffins are quick and easy to make and are the perfect complement to a coffee break. Here, they are made with chocolate chips and a mixture of berries (if you find them, add some stemmed fresh red currants), but you can also use chopped apricots or pitted cherries.

Makes 12 medium-sized muffins

8 tablespoons (1 stick) unsalted butter, at room temperature
2/3 cup packed light brown sugar
1 tablespoon mild-flavored honey
1 1/4 cups all-purpose flour
3 tablespoons Dutch-processed cocoa powder
1 1/4 teaspoons baking powder
pinch of salt
1 large egg plus 1 large yolk, beaten
1/3 cup plus 1 tablespoon milk
1/4 cup semisweet chocolate chips
1 cup mixed berries, such as raspberries, blueberries, and blackberries

Preheat the oven to 375°F.
Beat the butter, brown sugar, and honey in a bowl with an electric mixer until light and fluffy. Stir the flour, cocoa powder, baking powder, and salt together, and add to the butter mixture. Add the eggs and yolk, and mix. Gradually mix in the milk. Stir in the chocolate chips. Butter 12 cups of a muffin pan or line with individual paper liners. Fill each cup with equal amounts of the batter and then the fruit, pushing the fruit lightly into the batter.
Bake until muffins spring back when pressed in the center, 22–25 minutes. Cool slightly, then remove the muffins from the pan. Serve warm or, if desired, cool completely on a wire cake rack.

Chocolate apple cobbler

This chocolate cobbler is both easy to make and delicious, especially when served warm with a scoop of vanilla or cinnamon ice cream, or a spoonful of crème fraîche or creamy yogurt. In season, you can add fresh raspberries to the apples or replace them with a mixture of raspberries, blueberries, and stemmed red currants, sweetened to taste.

Serves 6

CHOCOLATE STREUSEL
1 cup all-purpose flour
1/3 cup packed light brown sugar
2 tablespoons Dutch-processed cocoa powder
1/2 teaspoon ground cinnamon
pinch of salt
7 tablespoons (3/4 stick + 1 tablespoon) unsalted butter, cut into small pieces, at room temperature
1/4 cup semisweet chocolate chips

Mix the flour, brown sugar, cocoa, cinnamon, and salt together. Add the butter and rub together with your fingertips until the mixture is crumbly. Mix in the chocolate chips. Refrigerate until ready to use.

APPLE FILLING
1/4 cup dark rum
3/4 cup raisins
12 Golden Delicious apples (about 4 1/2 lb)
4 tablespoons (1/2 stick) unsalted butter
1/3 cup granulated sugar
1/2 teaspoon ground cinnamon

Warm the rum, add the raisins, and set aside. Peel and core the apples and cut into slices about 1/3 inch thick. Melt the butter in a large skillet over high heat. In batches, add the apples until lightly browned, about 4 minutes. Return all of the apples to the skillet. Add the sugar and cinnamon and cook until the apples are almost tender, about 4 minutes more. Remove from the heat and stir in the raisins and the rum.

TO ASSEMBLE AND BAKE THE CRUMBLE
confectioners' sugar, for garnish

Preheat the oven to 400°F. Put the apple filling in a 2-quart baking dish, or 6 to 8 individual ramekins. Cover with chocolate streusel mixture. Bake until the apples juices are bubbling and the streusel is crisp, 20–25 minutes. Sprinkle with confectioners' sugar just before serving.

Chocolate and pistachio financiers

Financiers are very rich indeed, and it is appropriate that they are shaped like gold ingots. These small, oval or rectangular sponge cakes are delicious served as a snack or with coffee at the end of a meal. Large cakes can also be made with the same mixture, and are traditionally decorated with slivered almonds and candied fruit.

Makes 20 financiers

1$1/4$ cups (2$1/2$ sticks) unsalted butter
2$3/4$ cups confectioners' sugar
1$3/4$ cups almond flour
$3/4$ cup plus 2 tablespoons all-purpose flour
10 large egg whites, at room temperature
3 tablespoons Dutch-processed cocoa powder
$1/4$ cup pistachio paste

Cook the butter in a saucepan until it is a light nut-brown in color. Strain through a wire strainer to remove the browned particles.
In a separate bowl mix the confectioners' sugar, almond flour, and flour. Gradually whisk in the egg whites. Gradually stir in the melted butter until the batter is smooth. Place two-thirds of the batter in a bowl, add the cocoa, and whisk until combined. Whisk the pistachio paste into the plain batter until combined.

TO BAKE THE FINANACIERS
Preheat the oven to 400°F.
Butter 20 financier molds, 3$1/2$ inches long by 1$1/2$ inches wide and 1 inch deep. (To make the very small financiers in the photograph, use miniature financier molds, 2 x 1 x $7/16$ inches, and bake in three batches.) Spoon the two batters into the molds, using twice as much chocolate as pistachio. Lightly swirl the two flavors together with the tip of a small knife to create a marbled effect.
Bake until the financiers are lightly browned and spring back when pressed on top, 15–20 minutes (less for the small molds). Remove from the oven and immediately unmold the financiers. Cool completely on a wire cake rack.

Chocolate orange Breton sablé

This Breton sablé tart is as sweet in appearance as it is in taste. Its contrasting textures—the creamy smoothness of the pastry cream and crunchiness of the sablé, highlighted by the freshness of the oranges—combine to create the perfect after-dinner treat. Serve with a Gewürztraminer Vendange Tardive, a late-harvest wine from Alsace, for an even more enjoyable experience.

Serves 6

RICH SABLÉ PASTRY
1¼ cups all-purpose flour
2 teaspoons baking powder
pinch of salt
3 large egg yolks
½ cup sugar
7 tablespoons unsalted butter, at room temperature

Sift the flour, baking powder, and salt together. Beat the egg yolks and sugar with an electric beater until light and fluffy. When the eggs are well beaten, beat in the softened butter. Add the flour mixture and stir just until combined. Shape into a disc, wrap in plastic wrap, and refrigerate until well chilled, at least 3 hours.
Butter a 8½-inch tart pan. Roll the pastry out ⅛-inch thick and cut out a 12 inch round. Line the tart pan with the pastry round. Fold the pastry over so the folded edge is parallel to the edge of the pan. Prick the pastry shell with a fork. Freeze for 20 minutes.
Preheat the oven to 325°F. Place the pan on a baking sheet. Line the pastry shell with a round of baking parchment, and fill with pastry weights or dried beans. Bake until the pastry is set, about 15 minutes. Carefully remove the paper and weights, and bake until the shell is golden brown, about 10 minutes longer. Remove from the oven and cool completely on a wire rack.

CHOCOLATE PASTRY CREAM
2 oz bittersweet chocolate, chopped
1¼ cups pastry cream (see page 5 in booklet)
2 tablespoons heavy cream

Add the chocolate to the warm pastry cream. Let it stand until the chocolate melts. Add the heavy cream and whisk until smooth. Spread evenly over the cooled pastry shell.

TO ASSEMBLE THE TART
6 navel oranges
candied orange peel
chocolate shavings
confectioners' sugar

Cut the peel and pith from the oranges. Working over a bowl, cut between the membranes to separate the segments. Arrange the orange segments in concentric circles on the pastry cream. Garnish with a few pieces of candied orange peel and some chocolate shavings. Finish with a sprinkling of confectioners' sugar around the edge of the crust, forming a border about ¼ inch wide. Remove the tart from the pan. If you prefer, make 6 individual tarts rather than 1 large one.

Gluttony

"Lord! Who has not eaten a
little more than is strictly necessary?"

—Saint Augustine

Chocolate spice cake
(pain d'épices)

Although generally regarded as the French equivalent of gingerbread, pain d'épices (literally "spice bread") is a cake made from flour, honey, and spices and does not necessarily contain ginger. Premixed pumpkin pie spices can be found at any supermarket, but you can personalize your cake by creating your own mixture. All you need is a little ground cinnamon, cloves, cardamom, and ginger. Serve with an old Armagnac or Cognac to bring out the flavor of the spices.

Serves 8

3/4 cup wildflower honey
13/4 cups all-purpose flour
1/2 cup rye flour
1/4 cup Dutch-processed cocoa powder
2 teaspoons baking powder
2 teaspoons pumpkin pie spice or 1/2 teaspoon each
of the spices listed above
1 large egg
1/2 cup packed dark brown sugar
1/2 cup milk
5 tablespoons (1/2 cup + 1 tablespoon) unsalted butter,
softened

Preheat the oven to 350°F.
Bring the honey to a boil, remove from the heat, and cool to lukewarm. Sift the flour and rye flour, cocoa powder, baking powder, and spices together into a bowl. In a separate, larger bowl, beat the sugar and egg with an electric mixer on high speed until pale yellow. Add the milk and butter, and then the warm honey. Stir in the dry ingredients and mix well until smooth.
Butter and flour an 8-inch square baking pan. You can vary the shape of your spice cake by using differently shaped pans—a 9 inch long by 5 inch wide loaf pan works well, too. Bake until a wooden toothpick inserted in the center of the cake comes out clean, about 40 minutes. Unmold the cake onto a wire cake rack and cool completely.

Chocolate and hazelnut croquettes

These small, crunchy petit-four cookies go wonderfully well with tea or coffee. Here, they are baked into rounds, but they can be made in other shapes, such as diamonds and rectangles. Note that the dough needs to chill for a few hours before baking. If you prefer, you can replace the hazelnuts with almonds.

Makes 40–50 cookies

3/4 cup whole hazelnuts
12 tablespoons (1 1/2 sticks) unsalted butter, at room temperature
1 3/4 cups all-purpose flour
3/4 cup confectioners' sugar
3 tablespoons Dutch-processed cocoa powder
pinch of salt
1 large egg + 1 large egg yolk, beaten

Heat the oven to 375°F.
Spread the hazelnuts in a baking pan and bake until the skins are cracked, about 10 minutes. Remove from the oven and cool. Rub the nuts together in a kitchen towel to remove as much of the skins as possible. Coarsely chop the nuts.
Rub the butter into the flour with your fingertips until the mixture is crumbly. Mix in the sugar, cocoa, and salt, then add the egg mixture. Stir just until combined—do not overwork the dough. Mix in the hazelnuts.
Shape the dough into 3 or 4 logs about 1 1/4 inches in diameter. Wrap each in plastic wrap and refrigerate until firm and chilled, about 4 hours.
When ready to bake the cookies, preheat the oven to 350°F. Unwrap the dough logs and cut them into rounds about 1/4 inch thick. Place the rounds about 1 inch apart on a baking sheet lined with baking parchment. Bake until the cookies are crisp around the edges, 12-15 minutes.

Charlotte

This classic French dessert is made in a special tall mold lined with lightly soaked ladyfingers, and filled with mousse or stewed fruits. The chocolate version is fabulously indulgent and perfect for entertaining, as it must chill for a few hours before serving. Serve with custard sauce, or a whirl of whipped cream.

Serves 6

1/2 cup water
1/2 cup dark rum
1/2 cup granulated sugar
One 7-ounce package crisp ladyfingers (savoiardi)
11 oz bittersweet chocolate, chopped
12 tablespoons (1 stick) unsalted butter, cut into small pieces, at room temperature
5 large eggs, separated, plus 1 large egg white, at room temperature
chocolate shavings

Mix the water, rum, and 1/4 cup of sugar in a shallow dish to dissolve the sugar. One at a time, dip about 20 ladyfingers in the rum mixture, just long enough for them to color—they should not be soggy—and line the sides of a 7-inch diameter charlotte mold with the ladyfingers, placing the cookies rounded sides out. Dip some of the remaining ladyfingers and line the bottom of the mold, breaking them to fit. Set the remaining ladyfingers and rum mixture aside.
Melt the chocolate in a heatproof bowl set over a pan of barely simmering water (the bowl must not touch the water). Whisk in the butter, a few pieces at a time, whisking until smooth. Remove from the heat and whisk in the yolks, one at a time.

Beat the egg whites just until they form stiff peaks, adding the remaining 1/4 cup of sugar about halfway through. Stir about one-fourth of the beaten egg whites into the chocolate mixture, then fold in the remaining whites.
Pour the chocolate mousse into the mold and smooth the top. Trim the ends of the ladyfingers flush with the top of the mousse and scatter them over the mousse. Dip the remaining ladyfingers, break them up, and scatter over the mousse as well. Cover with plastic wrap and refrigerate until the mousse is set, about 4 hours. Remove the charlotte from the mold by turning out onto a serving plate. If it refuses to unmold, dip the mold for a few seconds in a bowl of hot water. Decorate with chocolate shavings.

Chocolate-chip brioches

Brioches are one of the most popular pastries in France and come in various forms, depending on the region. The brioches in this recipe can be eaten for breakfast or a snack, and are especially delightful served warm with a cup of creamy hot chocolate. They can also be sliced and dipped in a mixture of beaten egg yolk and milk, then sautéed in butter and sprinkled with sugar for the ultimate "French" twist.

Makes 2 brioches

1/3 cup milk, heated to 105°-115°F
2 x 1/4 oz envelopes instant yeast
2 cups all-purpose flour
3 large eggs, at room temperature
2 tablespoons sugar
1/2 teaspoon salt
12 tablespoons (11/2 sticks) unsalted butter, thinly sliced, at room temperature
1/2 cup semisweet chocolate chips

Put the milk and yeast in the bowl of a heavy-duty electric mixer. Let stand 5 minutes, then whisk to dissolve the yeast. Add the flour, eggs, sugar, and salt and stir to combine.
Mix with the dough hook attachment on medium speed until the dough mostly comes away from the sides of the bowl but is still sticking to the bottom, about 10 minutes. Do not add more flour—the dough should be very sticky.
One piece at a time, mix in the butter, waiting until the first piece is incorporated until adding the next piece. Knead until the dough cleans the sides of the bowl again. Mix in the chocolate chips.
Leave the dough in the mixer bowl and scrape down the sides. Cover with plastic wrap. Let stand in a warm place until doubled in volume, about 1 hour (if you have the time, the dough will be easier to handle if refrigerated overnight).
Lightly butter two 7-inch wide brioche molds. Turn the dough out on a well floured work surface—the dough will be velvety soft. Cut the dough in half. Using floured hands, loosely shape half of the dough into a ball and place in a mold. Pinch the top third of the dough to make a top-knot, but do not pinch the dough all the way through. Repeat with the other half of dough.

GLAZE
2 large egg yolks
2 teaspoons milk
pinch of salt

Whisk the yolks, milk, and salt to combine. Brush the brioches with some of the glaze. Cover each loosely with oiled plastic wrap, oiled side down. Let stand until the dough has doubled in volume, about 30 minutes (chilled dough will take 11/2- 2 hours).
Preheat the oven to 400°F. Using wet scissors, snip the crease of each brioche where the top knot meets the body. Brush the brioches again with the glaze. Bake until the brioches are golden brown (if the brioches are browning too quickly, reduce the heat to 350°F), 25-30 minutes. Let stand 5 minutes, then unmold onto wire cake racks. Serve warm or cool completely.

Chocolate-nut cookies

These cookies can be flavored with a variety of ingredients—pecans or macadamia nuts, candied orange peel, walnuts, raisins, or chocolate chips. They are even more delicious when served warm and slightly soft in the center.

Makes about 5 dozen cookies

14 tablespoons (1³/4 sticks) unsalted butter, at room temperature
1¹/2 cups confectioners' sugar
1 cup soft dark brown sugar
2 large eggs, at room temperature
3¹/4 cups all-purpose flour
1 teaspoon baking soda
¹/2 teaspoon salt
10 oz bittersweet chocolate
1 cup whole blanched almonds
1 cup walnuts

Preheat the oven to 350°F.
Beat the butter, confectioners' sugar, and brown sugar until light and fluffy. Beat in the eggs, one at a time. Sift the flour, baking soda, and salt, and stir into the butter mixture.
Coarsely chop the chocolate, almonds, and walnuts. Mix them into the dough. Shape the dough into logs about 2 inches in diameter. Wrap each in plastic wrap and refrigerate until chilled and firm, about 2 hours. Unwrap the dough and cut into rounds about ¹/2 inch thick. Place 1 inch apart on a baking sheet lined with baking parchment.
Bake until golden brown, about 12 minutes. (If you like chewy cookies, bake just until the edges are lightly browned, about 10 minutes.) Transfer to a wire cake rack and cool. Store in an airtight container.

Brownies

The secret of success when making these popular cakes is to cook them for exactly the right amount of time. If they are overcooked, they dry out and lose their soft, creamy texture—they should be only just cooked in the center. They are delicious warm, either on their own or with a scoop of vanilla ice cream or a spoonful of crème fraîche.

Makes 20 brownies

7 oz bittersweet chocolate, chopped
1½ cups (3 sticks) unsalted butter, at room temperature
6 large eggs, at room temperature
¾ cup granulated sugar
1 cup packed dark brown sugar
1⅓ cups all-purpose flour
1½ cups chopped walnuts
walnut halves
confectioners' sugar

Melt the chocolate in a heatproof bowl set over a pan of barely simmering water (the bowl must not touch the water). Add the butter and whisk until smooth. Whisk in the eggs, one at a time, then the sugar. Add the flour and stir until smooth. Stir in the walnuts. Spread in a 13 inches long by 9 inches wide baking pan, lined on the bottom with baking parchment.
Bake just until a toothpick inserted in the center of the brownie comes out with a moist crumb, 18–20 minutes. Cool in the pan on a wire cake rack. Invert to unmold the entire brownie, peel off the paper, and cut into 20 pieces. Decorate each brownie with a walnut half and/or a dusting of confectioners' sugar.

Gâteau de Nany

This recipe makes an ideal birthday cake—children love it! Quick and simple to prepare, it can be baked in different types of pans to produce all kinds of shapes, covered with ready-made or homemade frosting, and topped with chocolate icing or whipped cream.

Serves 6

8 oz bittersweet chocolate, chopped
7 large eggs, separated, at room temperature
1½ cups granulated sugar
13 tablespoons (1½ sticks + 1 tablespoon)unsalted butter, softened
1⅓ cups all-purpose flour
confectioners' sugar

Preheat the oven to 350°F.

Melt the chocolate in a microwave or in a bowl set over a pan of barely simmering water (the bowl must not touch the water). Cool until tepid.

Beat the yolks and sugar with an electric mixer until the mixture is light and fluffy. Add the butter and melted chocolate and mix until combined. On low speed, gradually mix in the flour.

Using clean beaters, beat the egg whites until they form stiff peaks. Stir one-fourth of the whites into the batter, then fold in the remaining whites with a rubber spatula. Butter and flour a 9-inch springform pan. Pour in the batter and smooth the top. Bake until a wooden toothpick inserted in the center of the cake comes out clean, 40–45 minutes. Cool in the pan on a wire cake rack for 15 minutes. Remove the sides of the pan and cool completely. Decorate with a simple sprinkling of confectioners' sugar, or more elaborately for those extra special occasions.

Index of recipes

The secrets of
Lionel Lallement

Lionel Lallement was never in any doubt about his chosen career and, at the age of 15, embarked upon an apprenticeship leading to a vocational training certificate that qualified him as a baker and pastry chef. He went on to win a number of prestigious professional awards, and in 1989, he was recognized as the Meilleur Ouvrier de France (MOF)—Best Craftsmen in France—in the pastry and confectionery division. At the age of 24, he became chef for Saint-Clair le Traiteur. He has remained loyal to the famous Parisian caterer and delicatessen, and every season produces a unique selection of pastries and confectionery that combines creativity and innovation.

PERCENTAGES IN CHOCOLATE

For some time, European chocolate manufacturers have prided themselves on the fact that the percentage of cocoa solids in their products is shown on the packaging. In fact the practice has become something of a marketing ploy, and people are taken in by it.

When manufacturers indicate a certain percentage of cocoa solids, say 60% or 75%, on a bar of chocolate, they are in fact suggesting and leading consumers to believe that the higher the percentage, the better the chocolate. This is simply not true. The percentage of cocoa solids shown on a bar of chocolate is the sum total of the amount of cocoa powder and cocoa butter contained in the bar.

For example, let's compare two bars of dark chocolate, one with 71% cocoa solids and the other with 66%. In the first instance, the actual composition of the chocolate is:
• 45% cocoa butter,
• 26% cocoa powder (for 71%),
• 29% sugar.
In the second, the actual composition is:
• 36% cocoa butter,
• 30% cocoa powder (for 66%),
• 34% sugar.

So it can be seen that the chocolate with 71% cocoa solids in fact contains less cocoa powder and more cocoa butter than the chocolate with 66%, and that the second bar of chocolate contains more sugar than the first. The cocoa butter primarily affects the texture and hardness of the chocolate—its effect on the flavor is incidental. The cocoa powder gives the chocolate its characteristics—acidity, bitterness, aroma, fruitiness, toasted quality, potassium content, etc. It can therefore be deduced that the percentage of cocoa solids is not an indicator of the quality of the chocolate, but only a part of its composition, which is often far from precise.

A WORD OF ADVICE
Consult an artisan chocolatier and listen to his advice and what he has to say about the origins of the chocolate he suggests. Just like a sommelier selecting a good-quality wine, the chocolatier will find you the chocolate of your dreams.

KEEPING CHOCOLATE FRESH

As everyone knows, chocolate is a fragile product that not only reacts with heat but also with air.

This is why most bars of good-quality chocolate sold in stores and supermarkets are first of all wrapped in foil to protect them from the heat, and then in a cardboard sleeve to protect them from the air and variations in temperature.

Exposed to the air, chocolate will automatically dry out, lose its aroma, its melting texture and its flavor. Remember that the flavors of chocolate are volatile and the less well protected it is, the more it loses its flavor. This is demonstrated by the fact that when you first open a box of chocolates, there is a very strong aroma.

This is why it is so important to buy freshly prepared chocolate. A good example of this is Easter—every year, chocolate rabbits and Easter eggs appear earlier and earlier on the supermarket shelves. An artisan chocolatier, on the other hand, will melt his chocolate at the last possible moment, pouring and assembling his creations as near as possible to the actual date in order to maximize their quality. If you go into a store that sells hand-made chocolates you will always be greeted by the delicious aroma resulting from the volatile flavors of freshly poured chocolate.

A WORD OF ADVICE
Buy your chocolate from an artisan chocolatier, freshly poured and made—the quality will be as good as it gets.

Keep chocolate in a dry place (61–64°F), wrapped in plastic wrap and stored in an airtight container to protect it from the air and humidity.

The secrets of Thierry Mulhaupt

Thierry Mulhaupt trained in Paris, working with some of the greatest French pastrycooks during the day and studying at the city's famous art college, the École des Beaux-Arts, in the evening. He won the Prix Jean-Louis-Berthelot in Paris, and first prize at the Olympiades de la Gastronomie in Frankfurt. His patisserie is conceived like a work of art in which flavors and decorations are composed with elegance and precision. He settled in the historic centre of Strasbourg in 1991, and in 1999 opened a store specializing in *pain d'épices* ("spice bread") and chocolates.

A GUIDE TO TASTING

I would like to try and describe a few key elements that will enable you to experience the maximum amount of sensations when tasting a chocolate. We have five senses at our disposal, and each can help us to make discoveries that are as wonderful as they are amazing.

Sight: start by considering the appearance of a chocolate. If it is light in color, it will contain less cocoa; if dark, it will contain more—the shades of light and dark vary according to the origin of the cocoa beans. You can also consider how shiny it is—a sign that it has kept well and also of the quality of the chocolate-making process.

Touch: a chocolate should be smooth, soft, and silky to the touch. Touch should be an integral part of tasting.

Hearing: plays a very small part in tasting, but when you break a bar of chocolate, there's a pleasant little snapping sound. If it is high pitched, it means that the chocolate has a high cocoa content or is relatively cold (and therefore too cold for tasting)—the ideal temperature is 20–21°C/68–70°F. If it is low pitched and dull, it means that the bar has a low cocoa content or that the temperature is too high.

Smell: when tasting chocolate, you can refer to the "nose" just as you would for wine. Before putting a chocolate in your mouth, hold it to your nose and inhale gently. This gives you an idea of the dominant aromas of cocoa, and secondary aromas such as spices, wood, toasted or earthy qualities, tobacco, leather, and even, for a certain variety of cocoa, petroleum.

Taste: when you taste chocolate, it is very important to chew it well. It has to melt in your mouth to release all the flavors. At this stage, we refer to flavors since what you taste in your mouth corresponds to three of the four existing flavors—sweet, bitter, and tart. You'll always find these three flavors in chocolate, but in different proportions depending on the cocoa content and origin of the beans.

When you swallow chocolate, the aromatic notes already experienced are confirmed by what is known as retro-olfaction—air exhaled through the nose. As with wine, you can refer to length on the palate or persistence in the mouth. The best type of chocolate should be long on the palate and have a good aftertaste. Just like wine, this can be measured in caudalies (a unit for quantifying persistence in the mouth of the flavors after tasting).

A good-quality chocolate should have a story to tell. It should be shiny, have a good aromatic palette, be tasty, full of flavor and, above all, have a good length on the palate. Occasionally I don't use any of the criteria to appreciate a particular type of chocolate, but wolf down a bar just because I feel like it. That's another thing about chocolate—you can enjoy it in any number of ways.

A FEW TASTING SUGGESTIONS

One final word of advice, enjoy your chocolate with a glass of wine, a liqueur or even a cigar for that complete chocolate experience.

Chocolate éclair	Good-quality mocha coffee
Dark chocolate 70% cocoa solids	Lapsang Souchong, a broad-leaved tea with a smoky taste and aroma
Dark chocolate 60% cocoa solids	A Criolos chocolate-flavored beer, brewed (in Alsace) with cocoa beans. It has an aroma and aftertaste of chocolate
Chocolate orange cake	Gewürztraminer 1989 (Jossmeyer SGN, Alsace)
Dark chocolate mousse with raspberries	Domaine de la Grange des Pères 1999 (Languedoc)
Chocolate tartlets	Noir de Grenache (Domaine des Mille Vignes, Fitou)
Dark chocolate 85% cocoa solids	An aged rum

The secrets of Henri Le Roux

The son of a Breton pastrycook who has lived and worked in the United States, Australia and France, Henri Le Roux was brought up in the world of cakes and pastries. After training in Switzerland, he settled in the French fishing port of Quiberon, in Brittany, where he opened a workshop and store selling hand-made confectionery and patisserie in 1977. His top-secret caramel and chocolate recipes brought him immediate success. Every year, the creator of caramel made with salted butter—*caramel au beurre salé* or CBS in French—adds other wonderful innovations to his repertoire, for example the dark-chocolate egg (Chítou) filled with a soft caramel made with butter and Belgian beer.

GANACHE

Ganache is an extremely delicate, creamy preparation with a melting texture made from chocolate and cream. It is used as a topping, filling, coating, or decoration for large and small cakes, sweets, and chocolate desserts. There are any number of ganache recipes whose main difference lies in the choice of flavoring.

But how is it that a ganache prepared under the same conditions, with the same ingredients and according to the same recipe, can have a different consistency each time you make it At the first attempt, you may produce a perfect ganache with a melting texture that is easy to serve, whereas the next time you are faced with a disappointing creation that is too soft, and therefore difficult to handle.

To ensure consistent results each time, always pour the mixture into the pastry case or mold at exactly the same temperature, i.e. 88–90°F. Then cover with plastic wrap and leave for 12 hours before serving.

A FEW WORDS OF ADVICE
WHEN MAKING A GANACHE
Choosing the chocolate: the type of chocolate depends on how firm you want the ganache to be. Always choose a chocolate with a higher proportion of cocoa powder and a lower proportion of cocoa butter. The cocoa powder contains the chocolate flavors, while the cocoa butter (which is white and is also used to make white chocolate) merely enriches and improves the consistency.

Confectioners' chocolate: as its name suggests, this chocolate is used for coating confectionery and cakes. Be careful if using confectioners' chocolate to make a ganache as it contains a higher percentage of cocoa butter—it consequently has very little taste and makes the ganache harder and fattier than it should be. It is the cocoa powder that contains all the delicate aromas of the chocolate, so if you do use confectioners' chocolate to make a ganache, you need to allow a larger amount of chocolate to obtain the same results.

WHITE CHOCOLATE

White chocolate only contains one component of chocolate—cocoa butter. It is a creamy white color and has little or no taste since it doesn't contain the other component, the dark brown cocoa powder that contains all the flavors of the chocolate. Strictly speaking, because it lacks the principal component, white "chocolate" shouldn't really be classified as a chocolate.

The secrets of Pierre Marcolini

Pierre Marcolini is a young Belgian chocolatier who has gained international renown. He has been passionate about chocolate since his childhood and has won some of the most prestigious international awards, becoming World Pastry Champion in Lyon in 1995, and European Pastry Champion in 2000. A valuable member of France's culinary community, Pierre Marcolini adds his own brand of creativity that has given rise to such innovations as cinnamon chocolates and petit-fours with mountain honey or tonka beans.

HOW TO MAKE A REALLY GOOD HOT CHOCOLATE

A traditional hot chocolate is made with 2¹/₂ cups milk to 9 oz chocolate. Choose best quality dark chocolate, with about 70% cocoa solids, made with Venezuelan cocoa (Caracas cacao).

Chop the chocolate finely with a knife or vegetable chopper to obtain fine shavings. Bring the milk to the boil with a vanilla bean, split open, or cinnamon stick, then remove the spices and pour the milk gradually onto the chocolate shavings. Add the milk to the chocolate in several steps, taking the time to whisk the mixture gently so that the shavings melt gradually.

TASTE DIFFERENCES BETWEEN DIFFERENT GROWTHS

Just as wine is classified according to growths (crus), each botanical variety of cocoa produces a specific growth, according to the conditions under which it is cultivated.

Criollo: a Mexican cocoa (cocoa of the Mayas), is the rarest and most delicate variety, representing less than 5% of world production. It has a heavily scented, fruity flavor and a subtle aroma that varies from region to region and from year to year.

Forastero: a cocoa from Upper Amazonia, is much hardier and has a fuller, more pronounced flavor. Cultivated in Africa, it produces fairly ordinary growths, but in Ecuador and Venezuela, the Equatorial climate gives it an incredible fineness.

Trinitario: a hybrid descended from a cross between Criollo and Forastero, it is cultivated in South America and Indonesia, with the best growths coming from Trinidad and Java. It has a fruity flavor and a good length on the palate.

Each variety has its own specific gustatory characteristics which are enhanced by a favorable climate and a relatively rich soil.

MAKING DARK, MILK, AND WHITE CHOCOLATE

Each of these three types of chocolate is obtained by means of the same process—the cocoa beans are cleaned, dried, crushed and roasted, then ground in mills to obtain cocoa paste (chocolate liquor).

The paste is then pressed to remove the natural fatty material (cocoa butter), leaving the cocoa cake (cocoa paste with most of the fat removed) that is ground to make cocoa powder.

Dark chocolate and milk chocolate are both made from a blend of cocoa butter and cocoa powder. Dark chocolate is made by adding a little sugar, vanilla, and soya lecithin. Milk chocolate has a lower cocoa content (around 30%) than dark chocolate and milk powder is added to give it its characteristic sweetness and smooth, creamy texture. White chocolate, on the other hand, is made by adding sugar and milk to the cocoa butter pressed out of the cocoa paste. It is the cocoa butter that gives the "chocolate" its white color. For this reason, certain purists don't regard it as a "proper" chocolate, but as a piece of confectionery made from cocoa butter.

The secrets of André Cordel

André Cordel was born in Verdun in northeastern France, and grew up in his father's bakery where he gained a vocational training certificate qualifying him as a baker and pastrycook. In the 1970s, he studied at the famous Coba school in Basle (Switzerland) and the École Lenôtre in Paris. He went on to practice his art at the Palet d'Or in Bar-le-Duc (Lorraine) and was acclaimed one of the great master patissiers by the Club des Croqueurs de Chocolat (Chocolate Crunchers' Club) and the Association of the Relais Desserts International. His imaginative chocolate creations include Bâtons des Maréchaux (marshals' batons), Renaissance, and Symphonie, a chocolate dessert that won first prize in the French National Pastry Championship.

ICED DESSERTS

An ice cream or sorbet is always a popular dessert, but it can be very disappointing when you serve your guests a scoop of ice cream that melts very quickly and ends up sliding across the plate. A trick of the trade that will help to avoid such problems is to put your plates in the freezer for a few minutes before serving the dessert. In this way, they'll be cold enough to stop it melting before it is eaten, and your iced desserts will be as good to look at as they are to eat.

CHOCOLATE MOUSSE

There are a few basic rules for making a successful chocolate mousse. Always use good-quality chocolate and exact quantities, and make sure the whipped cream is firm—but this is often difficult to achieve as the mixture of melted chocolate and cream slackens very quickly, even when mixed with the greatest care. The trick is to pour the chocolate and about 10% of the whipped cream into a bowl, cover with plastic wrap and bring to a boil in the microwave. Remove the mixture and leave to stand until it cools to a temperature of about 95–99°F. Then you can gently incorporate the rest of the whipped cream.
Served at room temperature, your mousse will be creamy and firm, but not fragile.

SALT YOUR DESSERTS

Add character to hot chocolate and melted chocolate desserts with a tiny pinch of salt. You'll be amazed by the result!

ADD CHOCOLATE TO SAVORY SAUCES

Preparing a sauce with red wine or a marinade to accompany game is not always that simple. Adding a small amount of very flavorful chocolate or, better still, cocoa paste (chocolate liquor) not only helps to bind the sauce but also makes the cooked wine a little less bitter. Leave to simmer for a long time to obtain a sauce that is extremely dark, shiny, and exceptionally smooth.

The secrets of
Sébastien Gaudard

Sébastien Gaudard grew up in his parents' patisserie and has worked and trained with a number of great pastry chefs. He served his apprenticeship with Georges Vergne in the Territoire de Belfort, a tiny region on the Franco-Swiss border, and then worked for two years with Gérard Banwarth at the Pâtisserie Jacques in Mulhouse. He spent eight years as pastry chef at Fauchon, the famous Parisian caterer and delicatessen, before working for three years as sous-chef to Pierre Hermé. On November 1, 2001, he founded a consultancy for patissiers-restaurateurs and, in 2003, opened Delicabar—the first Snack Chic—in the Bon Marché department store in Paris.

FLAVORING A GANACHE

Ganache is used for assembling macaroons, filling petits fours, truffles, chocolate, and cakes. It can be firm, thick, creamy, and even runny when used in chocolate sauce. It is a mixture of fatty materials contained in the chocolate and water contained in the cream, milk, and even the crushed fruit used to flavor it.It is the result of an emulsion that is very similar to the principle of making a mayonnaise.

The procedure for making a ganache remains the same whatever ingredients are added (honey, spices, pears, etc.).

To flavor a ganache, start by chopping the chocolate into small pieces. Put the required quantity of milk or a mixture of milk and heavy cream in a pan with the spices of your choice—Darjeeling tea (2–3 teabags), Tahitian vanilla (2 beans) or cinnamon (3 sticks)—and bring to a boil. Remove from the heat and leave to infuse for 3–15 minutes, depending on the required strength of the flavoring. Check the intensity of flavor before passing the liquid through a fine-mesh strainer—you should end up with the original amount of liquid (make up if necessary). Gradually pour the liquid onto the chopped chocolate, stirring with a balloon whisk, until you have a shiny, pliable mixture. Process in an electric blender to perfect the texture.

A SUCCESSFUL CHOCOLATE CHANTILLY CREAM

Here is a quick recipe that can't fail to impress your guests. It is made with $8^1/2$ fl oz whipping cream (35% fat) and one of the following:
• $5^1/2$ oz milk chocolate, 40% cocoa solids;
• $4^3/4$ oz confectioners' chocolate, 70% cocoa solids;
• 5 oz confectioners' chocolate, 64% cocoa solids.
You can also personalize this recipe by infusing the cream with any number of different aromatic ingredients (see "Flavoring a ganache" in left-hand column).

Three hours before you make the Chantilly cream, put the whipping cream in a pan and add the aromatic ingredient of your choice—for example, Earl Grey tea flavored with bergamot (2–3 teabags), mixed spice and chestnut honey to taste, ground Java peppercorns to taste, a few fresh mint leaves, or a few basil leaves and grated lime zest. Bring to a boil, remove from the heat and leave to infuse for 3–15 minutes, depending on the required strength of the flavoring. Check the intensity of flavor before passing through a wire strainer and chilling on the lower shelf of the refrigerator.

When ready to make the Chantilly cream, whip the cream until it is light and frothy. Melt the chopped chocolate in a microwave or in a bowl set over a pan of barely simmering water (the bowl must not touch the water). Add a quarter of the whipped cream and mix until you obtain a consistency similar to that of the cream. Reheat if necessary, then add the rest of the whipped cream. Finally, enjoy this smooth, shiny chocolate Chantilly cream with its delicately scented aromas.

The editor's acknowledgments
The editor would like to thank the following stores for their kind collaboration:
Agapé: pp. 32, 34, 36, 52, 60, 78, 84, 86, 92, 94, 100, 106, 112 / Anna Médeiros: p. 62 / Astier de Villatte: pp. 8, 12, 18, 28, 32, 58, 96, 114 / Créations Mathias: pp. 10, 30, 52, 74, 96 / Coquet: pp. 44, 62 / Côté bastide: pp. 26, 42, 44, 78, 84 / Cristal Saint-Louis: pp. 24, 114 / Deyrolle: pp. 6, 46 / Farfelus Farfadets: pp. 10, 12, 18, 28, 56, 62, 66, 80, 94, 96, 116 / Farrow & Ball: pp. 24, 32, 50, 52, 70, 78, 86, 94, 96, 114 / Fouquet confiserie: pp. 40, 52, 82, 86, 106 / Gaspari: pp. 16 / Mille Feuilles: pp. 44, 114 / Mokuba: pp. 24, 30, 32, 44, 64, 86, 94, 96, 114 / Nobilis: pp. 12, 44, 46, 64, 74, 78, 82, 84, 90, 96, 102, 112 / Pierre Frey: pp. 6, 26, 36, 66, 70, 96 / Point à la ligne: pp. 12, 18, 44, 78 / Samaritaine: pp. 16, 32, 36, 84, 92, 100, 102, 108 / Siècle: pp. 60, 70, 84 / Tissage de Luz: pp. 24, 86, 118 ;
Gontran Cherrier for his superb work and active participation in the project
Fabien Rouillard of Création Conseil Dessert (www.ccdessert.com)
for his help in creating and photographing the desserts
Gaëlle Moreno for her invaluable and very effective help

The designer's acknowledgements
Véronique Villaret would like to thank all the really lovely press attachées and designers who supported and encouraged her in the adventure of this first book, all the willing hands that worked so hard to make her task more enjoyable
Thomas, a great gourmet and a brilliant photographer
Gontran for so kindly making some really beautiful cakes
Jérémy and Aimery for their assistance, calmness and sense of humor
Gaëlle for her good nature and knowledge of packaging terms
Milou for a last-minute range of colored confectionery
Anne and Laurent for sharing their private, poetic world over a few sweetmeats
Anne and Pierre-Jean, for having faith in her and without whom she would not have put on those extra pounds of sheer heaven
And finally Samba for hands dusted with sweet cocoa powder

The photographer's acknowledgements
Thomas Dhellemmes would like to thank his wife, Valérie, who introduced him to indulgence
Véronique Villaret for everything she contributed with her brightly colored, poetic world
The entire Hachette team, especially Pierre-Jean Furet for his faith and the freedom he gave the photographic team
Anne la Fay and Gaëlle Moreno for their kindness and attention
His assistants, Aimery Chemin and Jérémy Zenou, two conscientious workers and real comics

Photographic credits
pp. 122, 123, 125, 126: DR; p. 124: Lorraine Le Roux; p. 127: Francesca Mantovani.

London, New York, Munich, Melbourne, and Delhi

Publishing Director: Carl Raymond; Executive Managing Editor: Sharon Lucas; Editorial Assistant: Nichole Morford; Art Director: Dirk Kaufman; Designer: Tai Blanche; DTP Coordinator: Kathy Farias; Production Manager: Ivor Parker

U.S. Recipe Adaptor: Rick Rodgers

First American Edition, 2006
05 06 07 08 09 10 9 8 7 6 5 4 3 2 1

Published in the United States by DK Publishing/Dorling Kindersley Ltd., 375 Hudson Street, New York, New York 10014

Originally published in France by Hachette Pratique under the title: les sept péchés du chocolat
Recipes by Laurent Schott
With the editorial collaboration of Pierre Jaskarzec
Photographs by Thomas Dhellemmes
Stylism by Véronique Villaret
© 2004 HACHETTE LIVRE (Hachette Pratique), Paris

American Translation © HACHETTE LIVRE (Hachette Pratique), Paris

ISBN: 0-7566-2290-5

Printed by Tien Wah, Malaysia

Discover more at www.dk.com